最新GRE
笔试模考练习

○ 本书编写组　编

中国环境科学出版社
·北京·

图书在版编目（CIP）数据

最新 GRE 笔试模考练习/本书编写组编.
—北京：中国环境科学出版社，2002.8
ISBN 7-80163-394-6

Ⅰ.最... Ⅱ.最... Ⅲ.英语-研究生-入学考试-美国-习题 Ⅳ.H319.6

中国版本图书馆 CIP 数据核字（2002）第 064722 号

出　版　中国环境科学出版社出版发行
（100036　北京海淀区普惠南里 14 号）
网　　址：http://www.cesp.com.cn
电子信箱：cesp@public.east.cn.net
印　刷　北京泰山兴业印务有限责任公司印刷
经　销　各地新华书店经售
版　次　2005 年 1 月第 4 版　2005 年 1 月第 1 次印刷
开　本　787×1092　1/16
印　张　13

定　价　24.00 元

目　录

教材说明

本GRE系列由《GRE类比·反义词教程》、《GRE填空教程》、《GRE数学教程》、《GRE阅读理解教程》、《GRE写作教程》和《最新GRE笔试模考练习》构成，由全国数十名著名GRE教学和研究专家历经数年集体编撰而成。

由于近年来GRE考试发生了一些变化，例如：作文改为机考了，语文、数学部分改在作文之后考了、词汇题也出现了不少新词，解题速度要求更高了等等。为了帮助广大同学适应上述变化，因此本系列涵盖了近十年的考试精华，尤其是涵盖了2002–2003年的最新考试趋势，真实地剖析和反映了ETS的出题思想及最新动态。

总之，本系列教材的实效性和实战性极强。广大同学只要使用本系列进行艰苦卓绝的训练，就一定能获得较理想的成绩。

2004年12月

一、最新GRE
笔试模考练习题一

SECTION 1
Time-45 minutes

ISSUE TASK

Present your perspective on the issue you choose from the two topics below, using relevant reasons and /or examples to support your views

Topic 1:

"Most people are taught that loyalty is a virtue. But loyalty—whether to one's friends, to one's school or place of employment, or to any institution—is all too often a destructive rather than a positive force."

Topic 2:

"The depth of knowledge to be gained from books is richer and broader than what can be learned from direct experience."

SECTION 2

Time-30 minute

Argument task

Discuss how well reasoned you find this argument.

The following is taken from the editorial section of the local newspaper in Rockingham.

"When XYZ lays off employees, it pays Delany Personnel Firm to offer those employees assistance in creating resumes and developing interviewing skills, if they so desire. Laid[a2]off employees have benefited greatly from Delany's services: last year those who used Delany found jobs much more quickly than did those who did not. Recently, it has been proposed that we use the less expensive Walsh Personnel Firm in place of Delany. This would be a mistake because eight years ago, when XYZ was using Walsh, only half of the workers we laid off at the time found jobs within a year. Moreover, Delany is clearly superior, as evidenced by its bigger staff and larger number of branch offices. After all, last year Delany's clients took an average of six months to find jobs, whereas Walsh's clients took nine."

SECTION 3

Time-30 minute 25 Questions

1. While scientists dismiss as fanciful the idea of sudden changes in a genetic code (spontaneous mutation), it is possible that nature, like some master musician, ____ on occasion, departing from the expected or predictable.
   (A) repeats
   (B) improvises
   (C) ornaments
   (D) corrects
   (E) harmonizes

2. Despite the ____ of time, space, and history, human societies the world over have confronted the same existential problems and have come to remarkably ___ solutions, differing only in superficial details.
   (A) continuity...identical
   (B) uniformity...diverse
   (C) actualities...varied
   (D) contingencies...similar
   (E) exigencies...unique

3. Although he was known to be extremely ____ in his public behavior, scholars have discovered that his diaries were written with uncommon ____.
   (A) reserved...frankness
   (B) polite...tenderness
   (C) modest...lucidity
   (D) reticent...vagueness
   (E) withdrawn...subtlety

4. With the ____ of scientific knowledge, work on the new edition of a textbook begins soon after completion of the original.
   (A) limitation
   (B) culmination

笔 记 区

(C) veneration
(D) certainty
(E) burgeoning

5. She is most frugal in matters of business, but in her private life she reveals a streak of ____.
(A) antipathy
(B) misanthropy
(C) virtuosity
(D) equanimity
(E) prodigality

6. If the state government's latest budget problems were ____ , it would not be useful to employ them as ____ examples in the effort to avoid the inevitable effects of shortsighted fiscal planning in the future.
(A) typical...representative
(B) exceptional...aberrant
(C) anomalous...illuminating
(D) predictable...helpful
(E) solvable...insignificant

7. Just as some writers have ____ the capacity of language to express meaning, Giacometti ____ the failure of art to convey reality.
(A) scoffed at...abjured
(B) demonstrated...exemplified
(C) denied...refuted
(D) proclaimed...affirmed
(E) despaired of...bewailed

8. WALLET: MONEY::
(A) bank: vault
(B) suitcase: clothing
(C) checkbook: balance
(D) wealth: prestige
(E) envelope: stamp

9. INSTRUMENTALIST: SYMPHONY::
(A) author: drama
(B) photographer: cinema
(C) composer: concerto
(D) artist: painting

笔 记 区

(E) dancer: ballet

10. PLATEAU: CHANGE:
(A) respite: activity
(B) asylum: security
(C) terminus: journey
(D) interval: time
(E) lull: rest

11. ISTHMUS: LAND::
(A) peninsula: island
(B) canal: river
(C) stratosphere: air
(D) strait: water
(E) tunnel: mountain

12. EMBARGO: COMMERCE::
(A) abstention: election
(B) strike: lockout
(C) boycott: development
(D) quarantine: contact
(E) blockade: port

13. DILATORY: PROCRASTINATE::
(A) recalcitrant: comply
(B) malcontent: complain
(C) ambivalent: decide
(D) inept: modify
(E) credulous: learn

14. NOMINAL: SIGNIFICANCE::
(A) titular: honor
(B) ephemeral: brevity
(C) divisible: continuity
(D) anomalous: distinction
(E) disjunctive: unity

15. PLAGIARISM: IDEAS::
(A) libel: words
(B) forgery: documents
(C) arson: buildings

笔 记 区

(D) kidnapping: ransom

(E) rustling: cattle

16. POLITIC: OFFEND::

(A) distressing: terrify

(B) aloof: associate

(C) misunderstood: surmise

(D) vacuous: deplete

(E) trivial: bore

Directions: Each passage in this group is followed by questions based on its content. After reading a passage, choose the best answer to each question. Answer all questions following a passage on the basis of what is stated or implied in that passage.

(This passage is from a book published in 1960.)

For many years, Benjamin Quarles' seminal account of the participation of African Americans in the American Revolution has remained the standard work in the field. According to Quarles, the outcome of this conflict was mixed for African American slaves who enlisted in Britain's fight against its rebellious American colonies in return for the promise of freedom: the British treacherously resold many into slavery in the West Indies, while others obtained freedom in Canada and Africa. Building on Quarles' analysis of the latter group, Sylvia Frey studied the former slaves who emigrated to British colonies in Canada. According to Frey, these refugeesâ2the most successful of the African American Revolutionary War participantsâ2viewed themselves as the ideological heirs of the American Revolution. Frey sees this inheritances reflected in their demands for the same rights that the American revolutionaries had demanded from the British: land ownership, limits to arbitrary authority and burdensome taxes, and freedom of religion.

17. According to the passage, which of the following is true about the African American Revolutionary War participants who settled in Canada after the American Revolution?

(A) Although they were politically unaligned with either side, they identified more with British ideology than with American ideology.

(B) While they were not immediately betrayed by the British, they ultimately suffered the same fate as did African American Revolutionary. War participants who were resold into slavery in the West Indies.

(C) They settled in Canada rather than in Africa because of the greater religious freedom available in Canada.

(D) They were more politically active than were African American Revolutionary

War participants who settled in Africa.

(E) They were more successful than were African American Revolutionary War participants who settled Africa.

18. Which of the following is most analogous to the relationship between the African American Revolutionary War participants who settled in Canada after the American Revolution and the American revolutionaries, as that relationship is described in the passage?

(A) A brilliant pupil of a great musician rebels against the teacher, but adopts the teacher's musical style after the teacher's unexpected death.

(B) Two warring rulers finally make peace after a lifetime of strife when they realize that they have been duped by a common enemy.

(C) A child who has sided with a domineering parent against a defiant sibling later makes demands of the parent similar to those once made by the sibling.

(D) A writer spends much of her life popularizing the work of her mentor, only to discover late in life that much of the older writer's work is plagiarized from the writings of a foreign contemporary.

(E) Two research scientists spend much of their careers working together toward a common goal, but later quarrel over which of them should receive credit for the training of a promising student.

19. The author of the passage suggests that which of the following is true of Benjamin Quarles' work?

(A) It introduced a new and untried research method-ology.

(B) It contained theories so controversial that they gave rise to an entire generation of scholarship

(C) It was a pioneering work that has not yet been displaced by subsequent scholarship.

(D) It launched the career of a scholar who later wrote even more important works.

(E) At the time it appeared, its author already enjoyed a well-established reputation in the field.

20. Which of the following can be inferred from the passage concerning Britain's rule in its Canadian colonies after the American Revolution?

(A) Humiliated by their defeat by the Americans, the British sharply curtailed civil rights in their Canadian colonies.

(B) The British largely ignored their Canadian colonies.

(C) The British encouraged the colonization of Canada by those African Americans who had served on the American side as well as by those who had served on the British side.

(D) Some of Britain's policies in its Canadian colonies were similar to its policies in its American colonies before the American Revolution.

(E) To reduce the debt incurred during the war, the British imposed even higher taxes on the Canadian colonists than they had on the American colonists.

Over the years, biologists have suggested two main pathways by which sexual selection may have shaped the evolution of male birdsong. In the first, male competition and intrasexual selection produce relatively short, simple songs used mainly in territorial behavior. In the second, female choice and intersexual selection produce longer, more complicated songs used mainly in mate attraction; like such visual ornamentation as the peacock's tail, elaborate vocal characteristics increase the male's chances of being chosen as a mate, and he thus enjoys more reprosuccess than his less ostentatious rivals. The two pathways are not mutually exclusive, and we can expect to find examples that reflect their interaction. Teasing them apart has been an important challenge to evolutionary biologists. Early research confirmed the role of intrasexual selection. In a variety of experiments in the field, males responded aggressively to recorded songs by exhibiting territorial behavior near the speakers. The breakthrough for research into intersexual selection came in the development of a new technique for investigating female response in the laboratory. When female cowbirds raised in isolation in soundproof chambers were exposed to recordings of male song, they responded by exhibiting mating behavior. By quantifying the responses, researchers were able to determine what particular features of the song were most important. In further experiments on song sparrows, researchers found that when exposed to a single song type repeated several times or to a repertoire of different song types, females responded more to the latter. The beauty of the experimental design is that it effectively rules out confounding variables; acoustic isolation assures that the female can respond only to the song structure itself.

If intersexual selection operates as theorized, males with more complicated songs should not only attract females more readily but should also enjoy greater reproductive success. At first, however, researchers doing fieldwork with song sparrows found no correlation between larger repertoires and early mating, which has been shown to be one indicator of reproductive success; further, common measures of male quality used to predict reproductive success, such as weight, size, age, and territory, also failed to correlate with song complexity.

The confirmation researchers had been seeking was finally achieved in studies involving two varieties of warblers. Unlike the song sparrow, which repeats one of its several song types in bouts before switching to another, the warbler continuously composes much longer and more variable songs without repetition. For the first time, researchers found a significant correlation between repertoire size and early mating, and they discovered further that repertoire size had a more significant effect than any other measure of male quality on the number of young produced. The evidence suggests that warblers use their extremely elaborate songs primarily to attract females, clearly confirming the effect of intersexual selection on the evolution of birdsong.

21. The passage is primarily concerned with
   (A) showing that intrasexual selection has a greater effect on birdsong than does intersexual selection
   (B) contrasting the role of song complexity in several species of birds
   (C) describing research confirming the suspected relationship between intersexual selection and the complexity of birdsong
   (D) demonstrating the superiority of laboratory work over field studies in evolutionary biology
   (E) illustrating the effectiveness of a particular approach to experimental design in evolutionary biology

22. The author mentions the peacock' s tail in line 8 most probably in order to
   (A) cite an exception to the theory of the relationship between intrasexual selection and male competition
   (B) illustrate the importance of both of the pathways that shaped the evolution of birdsong
   (C) draw a distinction between competing theories of intersexual selection
   (D) give an example of a feature that may have evolved through intersexual selection by female choice
   (E) refute a commonly held assumption about the role of song in mate attraction

23. According to the passage, which of the following is specifically related to intrasexual selection?
   (A) Female choice
   (B) Territorial behavior
   (C) Complex song types
   (D) Large song repertoires
   (E) Visual ornamentation

24. Which of the following, if true, would most clearly demonstrate the interaction mentioned in lines 8-9?
   (A) Female larks respond similarly both to short, simple songs and to longer, more complicated songs.
   (B) Male canaries use visual ornamentation as well as elaborate song repertoires for mate attraction.
   (C) Both male and female blackbirds develop elaborate visual and vocal characteristics.
   (D) Male jays use songs to compete among themselves and to attract females.
   (E) Male robins with elaborate visual ornamentation have as much reproductive

success as rivals with elaborate vocal characteristics.

25. The passage indicates that researchers raised female cowbirds in acoustic isolation in order to
(A) eliminate confounding variables
(B) approximate field conditions
(C) measure reproductive success
(D) quantify repertoire complexity
(E) prevent early mating

26. According to the passage, the song sparrow is unlike the warbler in that the song sparrow
(A) uses songs mainly in territorial behavior
(B) continuously composes long and complex songs
(C) has a much larger song repertoire
(D) repeats one song type before switching to another
(E) responds aggressively to recorded songs

27. The passage suggests that the song sparrow experiments mentioned in lines 37-43 failed to confirm the role of intersexual selection because
(A) females were allowed to respond only to the song structure
(B) song sparrows are unlike other species of birds
(C) the experiments provided no evidence that elaborate songs increased male reproductive success
(D) the experiments included the songs of only a small number of different song sparrows
(E) the experiments duplicated some of the limitations of previous field studies

28. STRINGENT:
(A) lax
(B) elusive
(C) impartial
(D) evident
(E) vast

29. INTERIM:
(A) obscure
(B) permanent
(C) prudent
(D) resolute
(E) secure

笔 记 区

30. SCATHING:
(A) easily understood
(B) politely cooperative
(C) intentionally involuted
(D) calmly complimentary
(E) strongly partisan

31. CAPITULATE:
(A) enjoin
(B) resist
(C) observe closely
(D) consider carefully
(E) appraise critically

32. RECONSTITUTE:
(A) detail
(B) invent
(C) spoil
(D) conform
(E) dehydrate

33. REPUTE:
(A) lack of caution
(B) lack of knowledge
(C) lack of emotion
(D) lack of generosity
(E) lack of distinction

34. TAME:
(A) resolute
(B) ruinous
(C) racy
(D) erratic
(E) experienced

35. INDURATE:
(A) soften
(B) puncture
(C) denude
(D) immure
(E) exchange

笔 记 区

36. PROLIXITY:

(A) succinctness

(B) profundity

(C) persuasiveness

(D) complacency

(E) cleverness

37. CALLOW:

(A) displaying keen intelligence

(B) behaving with adult sophistication

(C) reacting cheerfully

(D) showing foresight

(E) deciding quickly

38. FRIABLE:

(A) not easily crumbled

(B) not easily torn

(C) not easily melted

(D) not easily eroded

(E) not easily punctured

笔 记 区

SECTION 4

Time-30 minute 30 Questions

1. $\frac{1}{0.82}$ $\frac{1}{0.81}$

A rocket travels at a constant rate of 1 mile per second

2. The number of miles the rocket travels in 2 hours 10,000

$-x+4y=20$

$x-y=1$

3. x y

4. $2^{(2^3)}$ $(2^2)^3$

$0<n<1$

5. $\frac{4}{n+3}$

6. $2+\sqrt{2}$ $2\sqrt{2}$

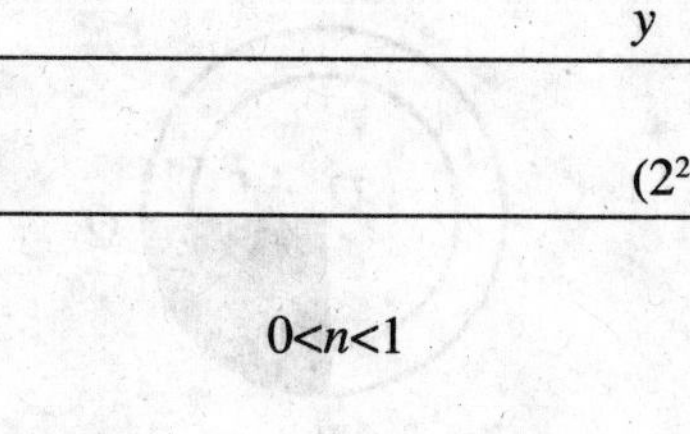

7. $r+v$ $s+t$

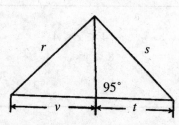

A grocer buys apples at the regular price of 38 cents per pound.

8. The amount saved by the grocer on a purchase of 100 pounds of apples if The additional amount paid by the grocer on a purchase of 100 pounds

笔 记 区

the price per pound is x cents less than the regular price	of apples if the price per pound is x cents more than the regular price

9. $2x+y$	$x+y$

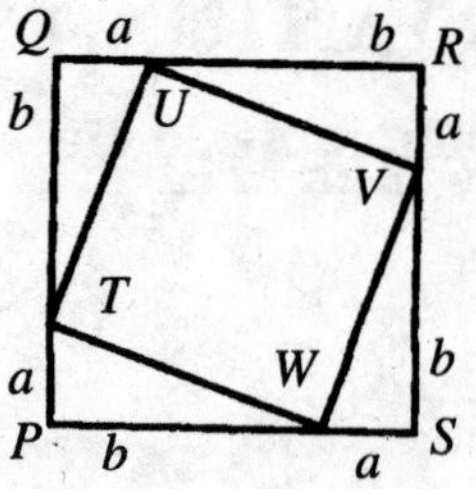

PQRS is a square

10. The area of square region *TUVW*	a^2+b^2

11. The median of the positive integers l, m, n, r, and s is 10, where $l<m<n<r<s$.

$\frac{l+s}{4}$	10

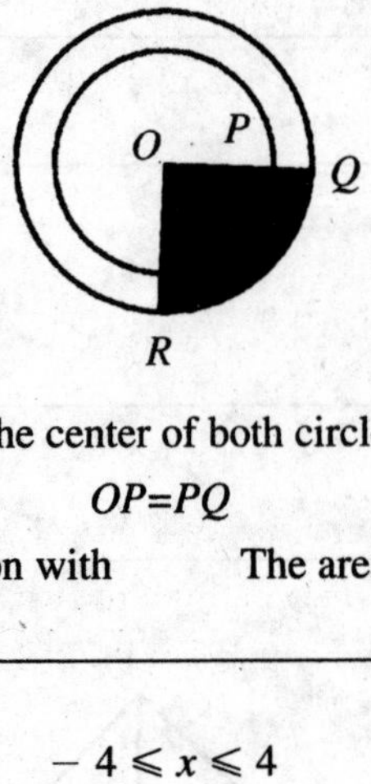

O is the center of both circles.

$OP=PQ$

12. The area of the circular region with radius *OP*	The area of the shaded sector *ROQ*

$-4 \leqslant x \leqslant 4$

$-8 \leqslant y \leqslant -4$

13. The greatest possible value of $25x - 12.5y$	200

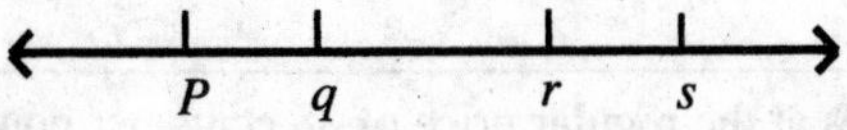

p, q, r, and s are the coordinates of the points indicated on the number line.

14. $p+q$	$r+s$

笔 记 区

$x \neq 0$

15. $-|-x|$ $-(x)$

16. If $3x+9y=7x+y$. then $8y=$
(A) $4x$
(B) $6x$
(C) $8x$
(D) $10x$
(E) $12x$

17. If the number of microbes in a test tube increases by 25 percent per day, how many microbes are there in the test tube at the end of a given day if the number of microbes at the end of the next day is 240,000 ?
(A) 180,000
(B) 192,000
(C) 210,000
(D) 288,000
(E) 300,000

18. The average (arithmetic mean) of five numbers is 88. Four of the numbers are 92, 89, 91...84. What is the fifth number?
(A) 82
(B) 84
(C) 86
(D) 89
(E) 92

19. The scores reported for a certain multiple-choice test were derived by subtracting 1/3 of the number of wrong answers from the number of right answers. On a 40-question test, if none of the questions was omitted and the score reported was 20, how many wrong answers were there?
(A) 5
(B) 10
(C) 15
(D) 25
(E) 30

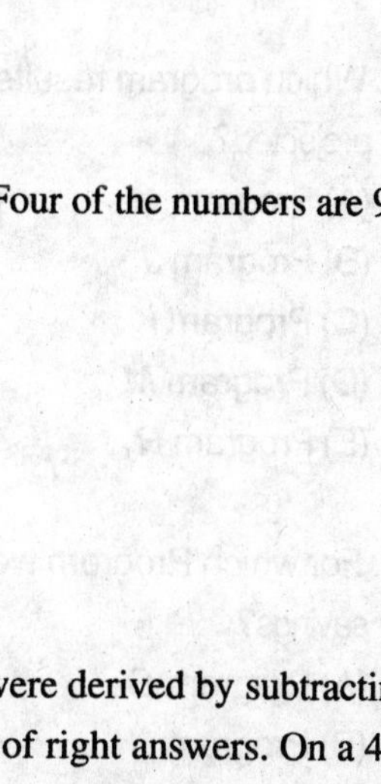

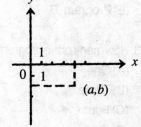

20. In the figure above, $a-2b=$
(A) -10
(B) -8

(C) 0

(D) 8

(E) 10

ACTUAL ENERGY SAVINGS AS A PERCENT OF PROJECTED ENERGY SAVINGS FOR EACH OF TEN PROGRAMS

Program	Energy Savings	Program	Energy Savings
G	36%	N	62%
H	45%	P	98%
J	107%	Q	72%
K	105%	R	109%
M	−12%	T	59%

Note: Projected savings were based on the expected decrease in use of kilowatt hours of electricity as a result of plants to cut demand for electricity

21. Which program resulted in an increase in energy use instead of a decrease as projected?

(A) Program *G*

(B) Program *J*

(C) Program *K*

(D) Program *M*

(E) Program *R*

22. For which Program were actual energy savings closest to 3/4 of the projected savings?

(A) Program *G*

(B) Program *H*

(C) Program *P*

(D) Program *Q*

(E) Program *T*

23. How many of the programs resulted in greater energy savings than were projected?

(A) One

(B) Three

(C) Four

(D) Five

(E) Eight

24. For which program was the ratio of actual energy savings to projected energy

savings closest to 1?

(A) Program G

(B) Program K

(C) Program M

(D) Program P

(E) It cannot be determined from the information given.

25. Actual energy savings for Program G were approximately what fraction of actual energy savings for Program T?

(A) 1/5

(B) 1/4

(C) 3/5

(D) 5/3

(E) It cannot be determined from the information given

26. If x is the sum of seven consecutive odd integers beginning with 3 and y is the sum of seven consecutive odd integers beginning with 5, then $y - x$ equals

(A) 2

(B) 7

(C) 8

(D) 12

(E) 14

27. If $\frac{5^{-1} \times 5^5}{5^4} = 5^y$, what is the value of y?

(A) 0

(B) 1

(C) 2

(D) 3

(E) 4

28. In a rectangular coordinate system, the set of all points (x, y) such that $-2<x<2$ and $-2<y<2$ comprises

(A) two perpendicular line segments

(B) two parallel line segments

(C) a circular region

(D) a triangular region

(E) a square region

29. The figure above shows a rectangular play area in which one child stands at B while another child runs back and forth along the entire side AD. If the running child is

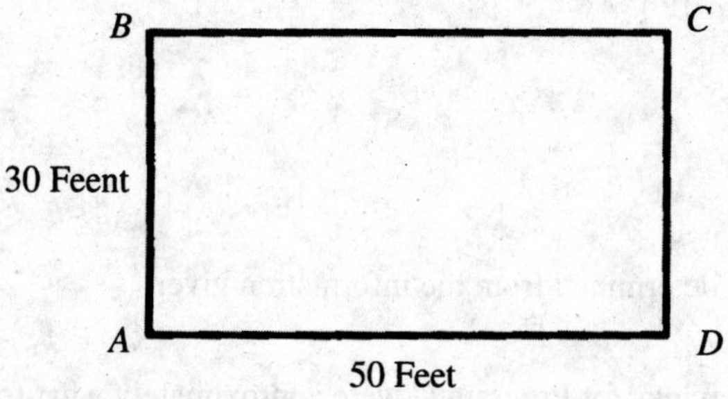

in a position randomly located along side AD at a given time, what is the probability that the two children are at most 50 feet apart at that time?

(A) $\frac{1}{5}$

(B) $\frac{2}{5}$

(C) $\frac{3}{5}$

(D) $\frac{4}{5}$

(E) 1

30. On a highway there is an electric pole every 96 feet. If the poles are numbered consecutively, what is the number of the pole 2 miles past pole number 56? (1 mile=5,280 feet)

(A) 109

(B) 110

(C) 152

(D) 165

(E) 166

SECTION 5

Time-30 minute 30 Questions

1. $\frac{9}{13}$ $\frac{90}{130}$

$x<10<y$

2. $x-10$ $y-10$

---

3. 10 percent of 25 percent of \$69.97 35 percent of \$69.97

$a=-1$ $b=2$ $c=3$

4. $\frac{a^2+b^2}{c^2}$ $\frac{1}{3}$

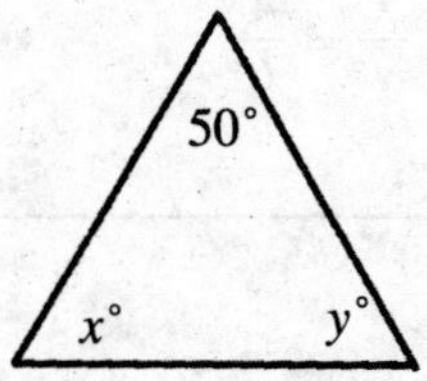

5. x 50

---

6. $\sqrt{26}+\sqrt{10}$ 8

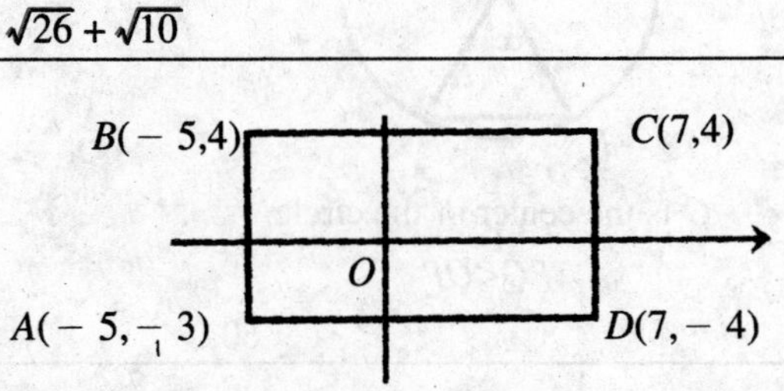

7. The area of rectangular region *ABCD* 84

$M(r, s, t)$ denotes the average (arithmetic mean) of r, s, and t, and $M(x, y)$ denotes the average of x and y.

8. M (70, 80, 90) | M (x, 90) where $x=M$ (70,80)

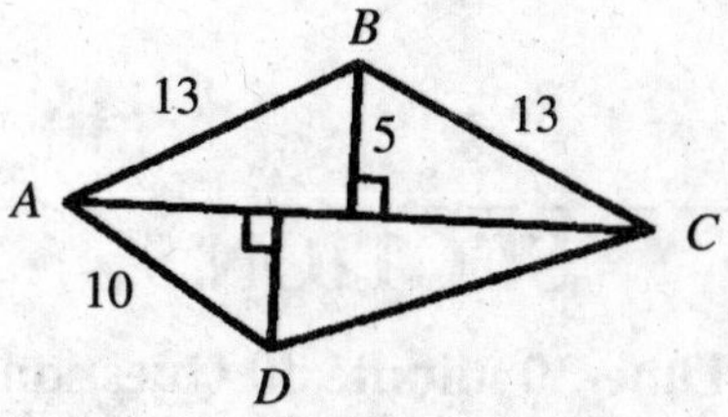

9. The area of triangular region ABC | The area of triangular region ACD

$$X^2+(2\sqrt{5})^2=6^2$$

10. $|x|$ | 4

$$x=y^2$$
$$1=cy$$

11. xc | y

Cylindrical tank X has radius 4 meters and height 3 meters. Cylindrical tank Y has radius 3 meters and height 4 meters.

12. The volume of tank X | The volume of tank Y

$$\frac{x}{y}=\frac{4}{6}$$

13. $y-x$ | 1

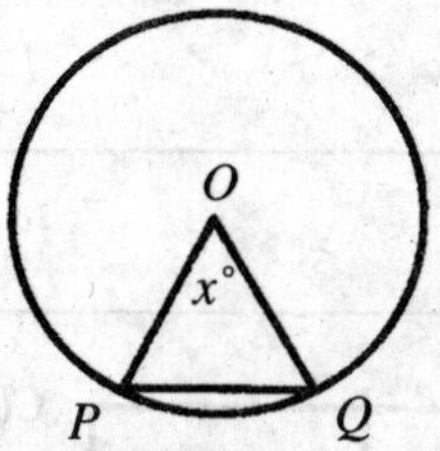

O is the center of the circle.

$PQ<OP$

14. x | 60

COMPARISON OF TEST SCORES FOR TWO CLASS

	Number of scores	Mean score	Median score
Class A	15	80	84
Class B	30	74	72

笔 记 区

15. The mean of the 45 scoresthe The median of 45 scores

16. If the temperature of a compound increases at a constant rate of 15 degrees per minute, how many minutes does it take for the temperature of the compound to increase from 60 degrees to 300 degrees?

(A) 12

(B) 16

(C) 20

(D) 24

(E) 30

17. If $\dfrac{12}{7-\dfrac{r}{s}}=2$, which of the following must be true?

(A) r=0

(B) r=6

(C) r=*s*

(D) r=2*s*

(E) r=3*s*

18. If the edges of a 3-inch by 4-inch rectangular photograph were each lengthened by 50 percent, what would be the area. in square inches, of the enlarged rectangular photograph?

(A) 18

(B) 20

(C) 24

(D) 27

(E) 30

19. If $\dfrac{x}{y}=2$ and $\dfrac{1}{x}=3$, then $y=$

(A) 1/6

(B) 2/3

(C) 1

(D) 3/2

(E) 6

20. Three pumps, *X*, *Y*, and *Z*. removed water from a tank. Pump *X* removed 550 gallons, pump *Y* removed 1,250 gallons, and pump *Z* removed 1/3 of the total number of gallons removed by the three pumps combined. How many gallons of water did pump *Z* remove from the tank?

笔 记 区

(A) 450

(B) 600

(C) 900

(D) 1,800

(E) 2,700

UNITED STATES FILM BOX OFFICE RECEIPTS AND AVERAGE ADMISSION CHARGE

1940—1990

Year	Box Office Receipt* (in millions of dollars)	Average Admission Charge
1940	$ 735.0	$ 0.24
1950	$ 1,376.0	$ 0.53
1960	$ 951.0	$ 0.69
1970	$ 1,162.0	$ 1.55
1980	$ 2,748.5	$ 2.69
1990	$ 5,021.8	$ 4.75

*Box office receipts are the total amounts collected from admission charges

21. For the year after 1940 in which box office receipts were less than they were ten years before, what was the average admission charge?

(A) $0.53

(B) $0.69

(C) $1.55

(D) $2.69

(E) $4.75

22. Which of the following is closest to the ratio of the average admission charge in 1950 to that in 1990?

(A) $\frac{1}{2}$

(B) $\frac{1}{4}$

(C) $\frac{1}{5}$

(D) $\frac{1}{9}$

(E) $\frac{1}{15}$

23. Approximately how many admissions were paid in 1940?

(A) 300,000

(B) 1,800,000

(C) 3,000,000

(D) 177,000,000

(E) 3,000,000,000

NUMBER OF FARMS IN THE UNITED STATES, 1850-1990

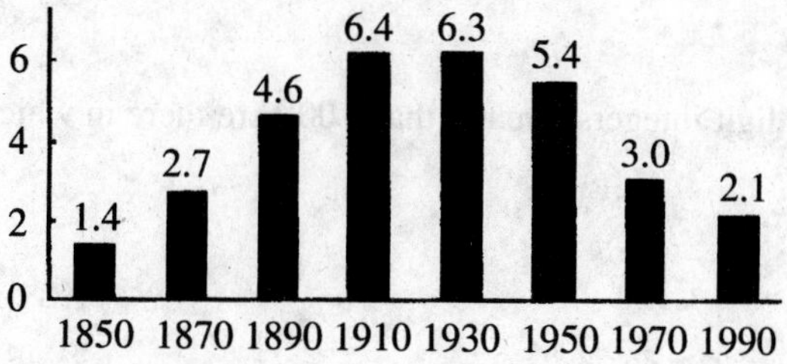

24. What was the percent decrease in the number of farms from 1970 to 1990?

(A) 9%

(B) 21%

(C) 30%

(D) 70%

(E) 90%

25. The average acreage per farm was approximately 140 in 1910 and 220 in 1950. The ratio of the total farmland acreage in 1910 to the total in 1950 was most nearly

(A) $\frac{3}{4}$

(B) $\frac{2}{3}$

(C) $\frac{3}{5}$

(D) $\frac{1}{2}$

(E) $\frac{2}{5}$

26. A research scientist wants to study a certain attribute of dogs. It is estimated that approximately 5 percent of all dogs have this attribute. If the scientist wants to study a sample of N dogs having the attribute, approximately how many dogs should be screened in order to obtain the desired sample size?

(A) N/5

(B) 5N

(C) 20N

(D) 105N

笔 记 区

(E) 120N

27. A square is inscribed in a circle. If the circle has radius 4. what is the perimeter of the square?

(A) 8

(B) $8\sqrt{2}$

(C) 16

(D) $16\sqrt{2}$

(E) $32\sqrt{2}$

28. How many 3-digit integers, greater than 100. Are there in which the sum of the digits equals 3?

(A) Three

(B) Four

(C) Six

(D) Nine

(E) Twelve

29. An equilateral triangle with perimeter p, a square and a semicircle were joined to form the figure shown above. What is the perimeter of this figure?

(A) 3p

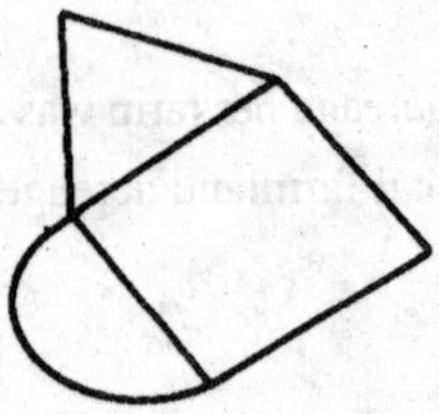

(B) $\frac{p}{2}+\pi p$

(C) $7p+\frac{\pi}{2}p$

(D) $\frac{7}{3}p+\frac{\pi}{3}p$

(E) $\frac{4}{3}p+\frac{\pi}{6}p$

30. If x is $11\frac{1}{9}$ percent more than y, then y is what percent less than *x*?

(A) 9%

(B) 10%

(C) $11\frac{1}{9}$%

(D) $12\frac{1}{21}$%

(E) 15%

SECTION 6

Time-30 minute 38 Questions

1. In spite of the fact that it is convenient to divide the life span of animals into separate stages such as prenatal, adolescent, and senescent, these periods are not really ____.
(A) advanced
(B) variable
(C) repeatable
(D) connected
(E) distinct

2. Although the number of reported volcanic eruptions has risen exponentially since 1850, this indicates not _____ volcanic activity but rather more widespread and record keeping.
(A) abating..detailed
(B) increasing..systematic
(C) substantial..erratic
(D) stable..superficial
(E) consistent..meticulous

3. The challenge of interpreting fictional works written under politically repressive regimes lies in distinguishing what is ____ to an author' s beliefs, as opposed to what is ____ by political coercion.
(A) innate...understood
(B) organic...imposed
(C) contradictory...conveyed
(D) oblique...captured
(E) peripheral...demanded

4. I am often impressed by my own ____ other people idiocies: what is harder to is that they, in their folly, are equally engaged in putting up with mine.
(A) analysis of...justify
(B) forbearance toward...underestimate

(C) exasperation with...credit
(D) involvement in...allow
(E) tolerance of...appreciate

5. Despite vigorous protestations, the grin on the teen ager' s face ____ her denial that she had known about the practical joke before it was played on her parents.
(A) belied
(B) illustrated
(C) reinforced
(D) exacerbated
(E) trivialized

6. Far from undermining the impression of permanent decline, the ____ statue seemed emblematic of its ____ surroundings.
(A) indecorous...opulent
(B) grandiose...ramshackle
(C) pretentious...simple
(D) ungainly...elegant
(E) tawdry...blighted

7. Despite the fact that it is almost universally ____, the practice of indentured servitude still ____ in many parts of the world.
(A) condemned...abates
(B) tolerated...survives
(C) proscribed...persists
(D) mandated...lingers
(E) disdained...intervenes

8. CANDY: SUGAR::
(A) chick: egg
(B) tire: rubber
(C) pen: ink
(D) mushroom: spore
(E) rag: scrap

9. SCRIPT: DRAMA::
(A) theater: play
(B) movement: symphony
(C) photograph: scene
(D) map: town

(E) score: music

10. AMBIGUOUS: UNDERSTAND::
(A) veracious: defend
(B) blatant: ignore
(C) prosaic: classify
(D) arcane: conceal
(E) plausible: believe

11. MERCURIAL: MOOD::
(A) callous: emotion
(B) doleful: energy
(C) jaundiced: attitude
(D) whimsical: behavior
(E) unversed: experience

12. PRISTINE: DECAY::
(A) adequate: imprecision
(B) stable: fluctuation
(C) volatile: force
(D) symmetric: flaw
(E) valid: exception

13. DIGRESS: EXCURSIVE::
(A) improvise: studied
(B) reiterate: redundant
(C) excise: prolix
(D) refute: plausible
(E) accede: contentious

14. PONTIFICATE: SPEAK::
(A) indoctrinate: preach
(B) impersonate: imitate
(C) obey: listen
(D) soar: fly
(E) strut: walk

15. OFFICIOUS: MEDDLE::
(A) disaffected: rebel
(B) bustling: excel

笔记区

(C) profligate: conserve

(D) subservient: esteem

(E) acrimonious: soothe

16. ATTENUATE: THICKNESS::

(A) separate: substance

(B) ventilate: circulation

(C) vaccinate: immunity

(D) transfer: location

(E) cool: temperature

An experiment conducted aboard Space Lab in 1983 was the first attempt to grow protein crystals in the low^{a2}gravity environment of space. That experiment is still cited as evi^{a2}dence that growing crystals in microgravity can increase crystal size: the authors reported that they grew lysozyme protein crystals 1,000 times larger than crystals grown in the same device on Earth. Unfortunately, the authors did not point out that their crystals were no larger than the average crystal grown using other, more standard techniques in an Earth laboratory.

No research has yet produced results that could justify the enormous costs of producing crystals on a large scale in space. To get an unbiased view of the usefulness of micro^{a2}gravity crystal growth, crystals grown in space must be compared with the best crystals that have been grown with standard techniques on Earth. Given the great expense of conducting such experiments with proper controls, and the limited promise of experiments performed thus far, it is questionable whether further experiments in this area should even be conducted.

17. According to the passage, which of the following is true about the Space Lab experiment conducted in 1983?

(A) It was the first experiment to take place in the microgravity environment of space.

(B) It was the first experiment in which researchers in space were able to grow lysozyme protein crystals greater in size than those grown on Earth.

(C) Its results have been superseded by subsequent research in the field of microgravity protein crystal growth.

(D) Its results are still considered by some to be evidence for the advantages of microgravity protein crystal growth.

(E) Its results are considered by many to be invalid because nonstandard techniques were employed.

18. It can be inferred from the passage that the author would find the Space Lab

experiment more impressive if which of the following were true?

(A) The results of the Space Lab experiment could be replicated in producing other kinds of crystals in addition to lysozyme protein.

(B) The device used in the experiment produced larger crystals on Earth than it did in space.

(C) The size of the crystals produced in the experiment exceeded the size of crystals grown in Earth laboratories using standard techniques.

(D) The cost of producing the crystals in space exceeded that of producing them using standard laboratory techniques.

(E) The standard techniques used in Earth laboratories were modified in the Space Lab experiment due to the effects of microgravity.

19. Which of the following can be inferred from the passage about the device used to grow crystals in the Space Lab experiment?

(A) The device is more expensive to manufacture than are the devices used in standard techniques in an Earth laboratory.

(B) The device has not been used to grow crystals in space since the Space Lab experiment of 1983.

(C) Crystals grown in the device on Earth tend to be much smaller than crystals grown in it in space.

(D) Crystals grown in the device in space have been exceeded in size by crystals grown in subsequent experiments in space using other devices.

(E) The experiments in which the device was used were conducted with proper controls.

20. The passage suggests that the author would most probably agree with which of the following assessments of the results of the Space Lab experiment?

(A) Although the results of the experiment are impressive, the experiment was too limited in scope to allow for definitive conclusions.

(B) The results of the experiment are impressive on the surface, but the report is misleading.

(C) The results of the experiment convincingly confirm what researchers have long suspected.

(D) Because of design flaws, the experiment did not yield any results relevant to the issue under investigation.

(E) The results of the experiment are too contradictory to allow for easy interpretation.

In 1923 the innovative Russian filmmaker Dziga Vertov described filmmaking as a process that leads viewers toward a "fresh perception of the world." Vertov's description of filmmaking should apply to films on the subject of art. Yet films on art

笔 记 区

have not had a powerful and pervasive effect on the way we see.

Publications on art flourish, but these books and articles do not necessarily succeed in teaching us to see more deeply or more clearly. Much writing in art history advances the discourse in the field but is unlikely to inform the eye of one unfamiliar with its polemics. Films, however, with their capacity to present material visually and to reach a broader audience, have the potential to enhance visual literacy (the ability to identify the details that characterize a particular style) more effectively than publications can. Unfortunately, few of the hundred or so films on art that are made each year in the United States are broadcast nationally on prime[a2]time television.

The fact that films on art are rarely seen on prime[a2]time television may be due not only to limitations on distribution but also to the shortcomings of many such films. Some of these shortcomings can be attributed to the failure of art historians and filmmakers to collaborate closely enough when making films on art. These professionals are able, within their respective disciplines, to increase our awareness of visual forms. For close collaboration to occur, professionals in each discipline need to recognize that films on art can be both educational and entertaining, but this will require compromise on both sides.

A filmmaker who is creating a film about the work of an artist should not follow the standards set by rock videos and advertising. Filmmakers need to resist the impulse to move the camera quickly from detail to detail for fear of boring the viewer, to frame the image for the sake of drama alone, to add music for fear of silence. Filmmakers are aware that an art object demands concentration and, at the same time, are concerned that it may not be compelling enough—and so they hope to provide relief by interposing "real" scenes that bear only a tangential relationship to the subject. But a work of art needs to be explored on its own terms. On the other hand, art historians need to trust that one can indicate and analyze, not solely with words, but also by directing the viewer's gaze. The specialized written language of art history needs to be relinquished or at least tempered for the screen. Only an effective collaboration between filmmakers and art historians can create films that will enhance viewers' perceptions of art.

21. The passage suggests that a filmmaker desiring to enhance viewers's perceptions of art should do which of the following?

(A) Rely on the precise language of art history when developing scripts for films on art.

(B) Rely on dramatic narrative and music to set a film's tone and style.

(C) Recognize that a work of art by itself can be compelling enough to hold a viewer's attention.

(D) Depend more strongly on narration instead of camera movements to guide the viewer's gaze.

笔记区

(E) Emphasize the social and the historical contexts within which works of art have been created.

22. The author of the passage refers to Vertov in the first paragraph most probably in order to

(A) provide an example of how films can be used to influence perceptions

(B) present evidence to support the argument that films have been used successfully to influence viewers' perceptions

(C) introduce the notion that film can influence how viewers see

(D) contrast a traditional view of the uses of film with a more modern view

(E) describe how film can change a viewer's perception of a work of art

23. Which of the following best describes the organization of the passage?

(A) An observation about an unsatisfactory situation is offered, the reasons for the situation are discussed, and then ways to change it are suggested.

(B) Two opinions regarding a controversial phenomenon are contrasted, supporting evidence for each is presented, and then the two opinions are reconciled.

(C) Criticism of a point of view is discussed, the criticism is answered, and then the criticism is applied to another point of view.

(D) A point of view is described, evidence supporting the view is provided, and then a summary is presented.

(E) A strategy is presented, reasons for its past failure are discussed, and then a recommendation that will be abandoned is offered.

24. The passage is primarily concerned with

(A) discussing why film's potential as a medium for presenting art to the general public has not been fully realized and how film might be made more effective in this regard

(B) discussing the shortcomings of films on art and the technological innovations required to increase the impact of film on visual literacy

(C) discussing the advantages and the disadvantages of using films rather than publications to present works of art to the general public

(D) presenting information to support the view that films on art must focus more on education and less on entertainment in order to increase visual literacy

(E) presenting information to support the view that films on art, because they reach a broader audience than many other kinds of media, have had greater success in promoting visual literacy

25. The author would most likely agree with which of the following statements about film and visual literacy?

笔 记 区

(A) Reading a publication about a work of art and then seeing a film about the same work is the most effective way to develop visual literacy.

(B) An increase in a viewer's awareness of visual forms will also lead to an increased attention span.

(C) Film has a great but not yet fully exploited capacity to increase viewers awareness of visual forms.

(D) A film that focuses on the details of a work of art will hinder the development of visual literacy.

(E) Films on art would more effectively enhance the visual literacy of teenagers if filmmakers followed the standards set by rock videos.

26. According to the passage, art historians desiring to work with filmmakers to enhance the public's appreciation of art need to acknowledge which of the following?

(A) The art historian's role in the creation of a film on art is likely to be a relatively minor one.

(B) Film provides an ideal opportunity to acquaint viewers with a wide range of issues that relate incidentally to a work of art.

(C) An in-depth analysis of a work of art is not an appropriate topic for a film on art.

(D) Although silence may be an appropriate background when viewing a work of art in a museum, it is inappropriate in a film.

(E) Film can use nonverbal means to achieve some of the same results that a spoken or written discourse can achieve.

27. Which of the following would describe the author's most likely reaction to a claim that films on art would more successfully promote visual literacy if they followed the standards set for rock videos?

(A) Ambivalence

(B) Indifference

(C) Sympathy

(D) Interest

(E) Disdain

28. ACCESSORY:

(A) insubordinate

(B) invisible

(C) of high quality

(D) of massive proportions

(E) of primary importance

笔 记 区

29. CHAMPION:
(A) emulate
(B) disparage
(C) compel
(D) anticipate
(E) disappoint

30. DECADENCE:
(A) cheerfulness
(B) promptness
(C) cleanliness
(D) wholesomeness
(E) carefulness

31. OPACITY:
(A) transparency
(B) smoothness
(C) colorlessness
(D) elongation and thinness
(E) hardness and durability

32. MISGIVING:
(A) consistency
(B) certainty
(C) generosity
(D) loyalty
(E) affection

33. HARANGUE:
(A) overtly envy
(B) intermittently forget
(C) gratefully acknowledge
(D) speak temperately
(E) sacrifice unnecessarily

34. GERMANE:
(A) unproductive
(B) irregular
(C) indistinguishable
(D) irrelevant
(E) unsubstantiated

笔 记 区

35. IMPUGN:
(A) rectify
(B) classify
(C) vindicate
(D) mollify
(E) chastise

36. INEXORABLE:
(A) discernible
(B) quantifiable
(C) relenting
(D) inspiring
(E) revealing

37. RESTIVE:
(A) necessary
(B) interesting
(C) calm
(D) healthy
(E) deft

38. BAIT:
(A) perplex
(B) disarm
(C) delude
(D) release
(E) fortify

二、最新GRE
笔试模考练习题二

SECTION 1

Time-45 minutes

ISSUE TASK

Present your perspective on the issue you choose from the two topics below, using relevant reasons and /or examples to support your views

Topic 1:

"Too much time, money, and energy are spent developing new and more elaborate technology. Society should instead focus on maximizing the use of existing technology for the immediate benefit of its citizens."

Topic 2:

"Instant communication systems encourage people to form hasty opinions and give quick replies rather than take the time to develop thoughtful, well-reasoned points of view."

笔 记 区

SECTION 2

Time-30 minute

Argument task

Discuss how well reasoned you find this argument.

The following is taken from the editorial section of the local newspaper in Rockingham.

"In order to save a considerable amount of money, Rockingham's century-old town hall should be torn down and replaced by the larger and more energy-efficient building that some citizens have proposed. The old town hall is too small to comfortably accommodate the number of people who are employed by the town. In addition, it is very costly to heat the old hall in winter and cool it in summer. The new, larger building would be more energy efficient, costing less per square foot to heat and cool than the old hall. Furthermore, it would be possible to rent out some of the space in the new building, thereby generating income for the town of Rockingham."

笔 记 区

SECTION 3

Time-30 minute 25 Questions

1. 60 percent of 16 10

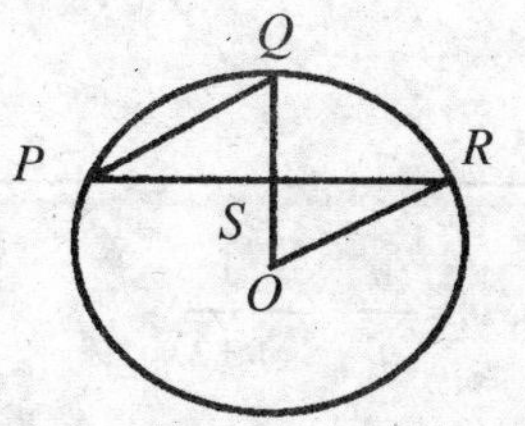

O is the center of the circle and $OS=SQ$.

2. PQ OR

n is an integer such that $1<n<4$.

3. $n-1$ 2

$$\frac{1}{2}x+9=20$$

4. $x+19$ 40

Board A measures between 2.15 feet and 2. 25 feet in length; board B measures between 2.20 feet and 2.30 feet in length.

5. The length of board A The length of board B

$$t^2-2t=0$$
$$t \neq 0$$

6. t 2

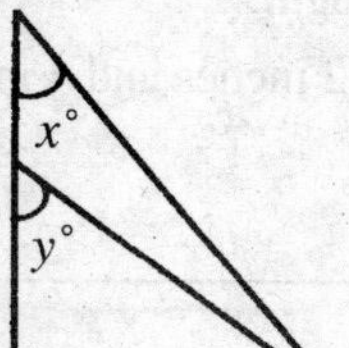

笔记区

7.	x	y
8.	$x\,(y+z)$	$xy+z$
9.	10^4	5^6

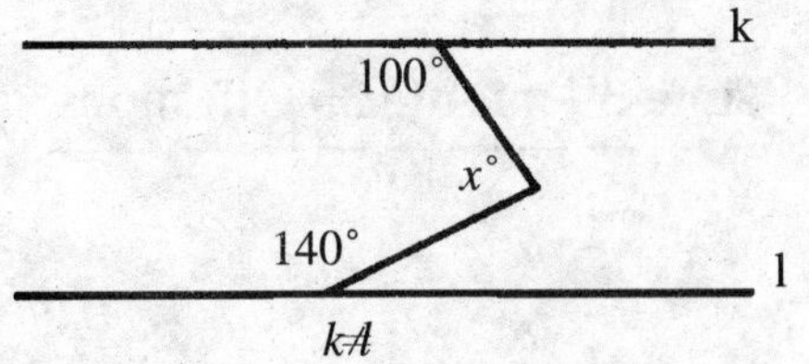

10.	x	120
11.	$(\frac{1.5}{2.5})^2$	0.36

For each positive integer n, $a_n=\frac{1}{n}\quad\frac{1}{n+1}$

12.	$a_1+a_2+a_3+a_4$	$\frac{4}{5}$

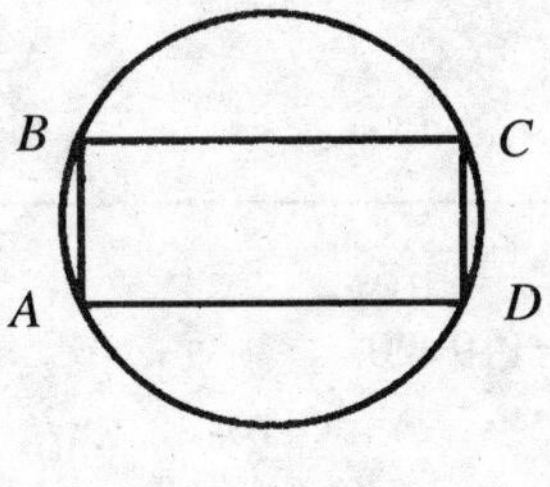

Tre radius of the circle is r.

13. The area of rectangular region $ABCD$

S is a set of n consecutive integers.

14. The mean of S — The median of S

The length of a rectangular box is 4 inches longer than the depth, and the width of the box is 1 inch less than the length.

The depth of the box is between 2 inches and 4 inches.

15. The volume of the box in cubic inches — 200

16. In a circle graph used to represent a budget totaling \$600, the measure of the central angle associated with a \$120 item in the budget is

(A) 72°

(B) 108°

(C) 120°

(D) 144°

(E) 216°

17. $(\frac{1}{2}-\frac{1}{3})+(\frac{1}{3}-\frac{1}{4})+(\frac{1}{4}-\frac{1}{2})=$

(A) 0

(B) $\frac{1}{4}$

(C) $\frac{1}{2}$

(D) 1

(E) $\frac{5}{4}$

18. The vertices of square *S* have coordinates (−1, −2), (−1, 1), (2, 1), and (2, −2), respectively. What are the coordinates of the point where the diagonals of S intersect?

(A) $(\frac{1}{2}, \frac{1}{2})$

(B) $(\frac{1}{2}, -\frac{1}{2})$

(C) $(\frac{3}{2}, \frac{1}{2})$

(D) $(\frac{3}{2}, -\frac{1}{2})$

(E) $(\frac{\sqrt{3}}{2}, \frac{1}{2})$

19. The admission price per child at a certain amusement park is $\frac{7}{12}$ of the admission price per adult. If the admission price for 4 adults and 6 children is \$112.50, what is the admission price per adult?

(A) \$15.00

(B) \$13.50

(C) \$12.75

(D) \$11.25

(E) \$8.75

20. If $x=2y$ and $y=2z/3$, what is the value of z in terms of x?

笔 记 区

(A) $\frac{2x}{3}$

(B) $\frac{3x}{4}$

(C) $\frac{4x}{3}$

(D) $\frac{3x}{2}$

(E) $3x$

<u>Questions 21-25</u> refer to the following graph.

INDUSTRLAL WASTE GENERATED BY
SPECIFIC INDUSTRIES OF COUNTRY X

<u>Note:</u> Because of the great disparity in the amounts of waste generated by different industries, the graph is broken in three places, and after each break, a new and more appropriate scale is introduced. As usual, the value represented by a bar is read only at its far right end.

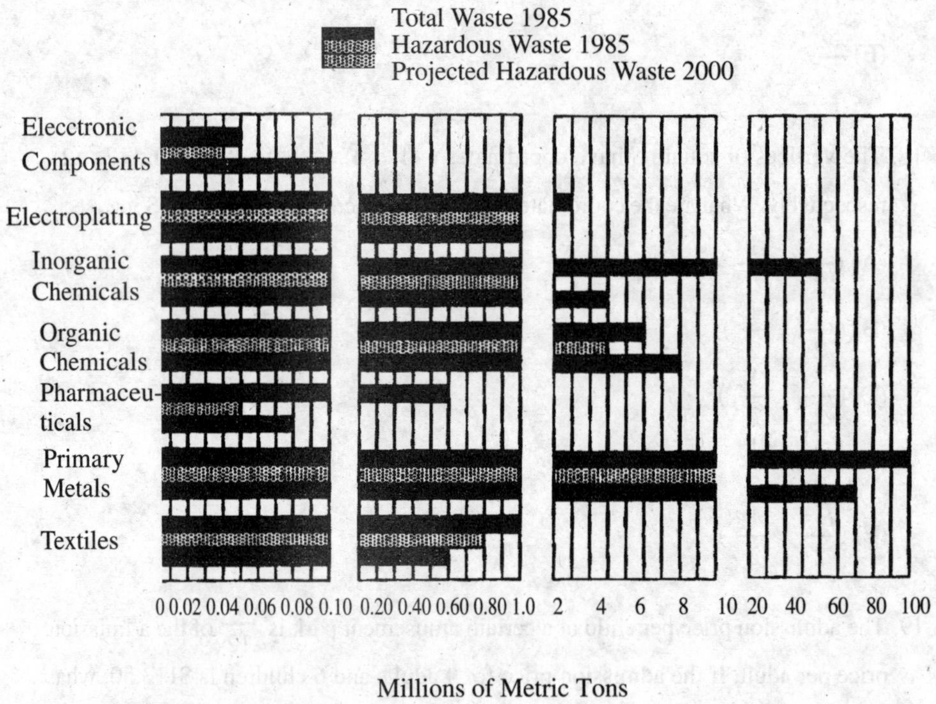

21. How many million metric tons of hazardous waste was produced in 1985 by the inorganic and organic chemicals industries combined?

(A) 66

(B) 16

(C) 10

(D) 5

(E) 3

笔 记 区

22. For those industries that generated a total of more than a million metric tons of waste in 1985, what was the approximate average (arithmetic mean) total waste, in millions of metric tons, generated per industry?

(A) 42
(B) 34
(C) 28
(D) 25
(E) 23

23. In 1985 hazardous waste in electroplating exceeded hazardous waste in electronic components by how many million metric tons?

(A) 1.96
(B) 1.50
(C) 0.96
(D) 0.80
(E) 0.60

24. In 1985 the pharmaceuticals industry generated total waste equal to how many times the hazardous waste in the same industry?

(A) 1.2
(B) 2.5
(C) 3
(D) 6
(E) 12

25. For which of the following industries is the hazardous waste projection for the year 2000 at least double its 1985 level?

I. Electronic components
II. Electroplating
III. Inorganic chemicals

(A) I only
(B) I and II only
(C) I and III only
(D) II and III only
(E) I, II, and III

26. Sixty-eight people are sitting in 20 cars and each car contains at most 4 people. What is the maximum possible number of cars that could contain exactly 1 of the 68 people?

(A) 2
(B) 3

笔 记 区

(C) 4

(D) 8

(E) 12

27. The width of a rectangular playground is 75 percent of the length. If the perimeter of the playground is 280 meters, how long, in meters, is a straight path that cuts diagonally across the playground from one corner to another?

(A) 60

(B) 70

(C) 80

(D) 90

(E) 100

28. Which of the following numbers is NOT the sum of three consecutive odd integers?

(A) 15

(B) 75

(C) 123

(D) 297

(E) 313

29. If $72.42 = k(24+\frac{n}{100})$, where k and n are positive integers and $n<100$, then $k+n=$

(A) 17

(B) 16

(C) 15

(D) 14

(E) 13

30. Which of the following pairs of numbers has an average(arithmetic mean) of 2?

(A) $2-\sqrt{2}$, $4-\sqrt{2}$

(B) $2\sqrt{3}$, $2-2\sqrt{3}$

(C) $\frac{1}{0.5}$, $\frac{2.4}{1.6}$

(D) $\sqrt{5}$, $\sqrt{3}$

(E) $\frac{\frac{1}{2}}{3}$, $\frac{\frac{1}{2}}{5}$

笔记区

SECTION 4

Time-30 minute 38 Questions

1. What these people were waiting for would not have been apparent to others and was perhaps not very_______their own minds.
(A) obscure to
(B) intimate to
(C) illusory to
(D) difficult for
(E) definite in

2. The attempt to breed suitable varieties of jojoba by using hybridization to _______ favorable traits was finally abandoned in favor of a simpler and much faster_______: the domestication of flourishing wild strains.
(A) eliminate...alternative
(B) reinforce...method
(C) allow...creation
(D) reduce...idea
(E) concentrate...theory

3. According to one political theorist, a regime that has as its goal absolute________, without any________law or principle, has declared war on justice.
(A) respectability...codification of
(B) supremacy...suppression of
(C) autonomy...accountability to
(D) fairness...deviation from
(E) responsibility...prioritization of

4. Despite its_________, the book deals_________with a number of crucial issues.
(A) optimism...cursorily
(B) importance...needlessly
(C) virtues...inadequately
(D) novelty...strangely

笔记区

(E) completeness...thoroughly

5. Although frequent air travelers remain unconvinced, researchers have found that, paradoxically, the______disorientation inherent in jet lag also may yield some mental health______.
(A) temporal...benefits
(B) acquired...hazards
(C) somatic...disorders
(D) random...deficiencies
(E) typical...standards

6. Ironically, the proper use of figurative language must be based on the denotative meaning of the words, because it is the failure to recognize this_____ meaning that leads to mixed metaphors and their attendant incongruity.
(A) esoteric
(B) literal
(C) latent
(D) allusive
(E) symbolic

7. Although it seems______that there would be a greater risk of serious automobile accidents in densely populated areas, such accidents are more likely to occur in sparsely populated regions.
(A) paradoxical
(B) axiomatic
(C) anomalous
(D) irrelevant
(E) portentous

8. CATASTROPHE: MISHAP::
(A) prediction: recollection
(B) contest: recognition
(C) humiliation: embarrassment
(D) reconciliation: solution
(E) hurdle: challenge

9. SONNET: POET::
(A) stage: actor
(B) orchestra: conductor
(C) music: dancer

笔 记 区

(D) canvas: painter

(E) symphony: composer

10. LOQUACIOUS: SUCCINCT::

(A) placid: indolent

(B) vivacious: cheerful

(C) vulgar: offensive

(D) pretentious: sympathetic

(E) adroit: ungainly

11. DEPORTATION:COUNTRY::

(A) evacuation: shelter

(B) abdication: throne

(C) extradition: court

(D) eviction: dwelling

(E) debarkation: destination

12. MAELSTROM:TURBULENT::

(A) stricture: imperative

(B) mirage: illusory

(C) antique: rare

(D) myth: authentic

(E) verdict: fair

13. ABSTEMIOUS: INDULGE::

(A) affectionate: embrace

(B) austere: decorate

(C) articulate: preach

(D) argumentative: harangue

(E) affable: jest

14. BLUSTERING: SPEAK::

(A) grimacing: smile

(B) blinking: stare

(C) slouching: sit

(D) jeering: laugh

(E) swaggering: walk

15. SOLACE: GRIEF::

(A) rebuke: mistake

(B) mortification: passion

笔 记 区

(C) encouragement: confidence
(D) justification: action
(E) pacification: anger

16. INDELIBLE: FORGET::
(A) lucid: comprehend
(B) astounding: expect
(C) inconsequential: reduce
(D) incorrigible: agree
(E) fearsome: avoid

Investigators of monkeys' social behavior have always been struck by monkeys' aggressive potential and the consequent need for social control of their aggressive behavior. Studies directed at describing aggressive behavior and the situations that elicit it, as well as the social mechanisms that control it, were therefore among the first investigations of monkeys' social behavior.

Investigators initially believed that monkeys would compete for any resource in the environment: hungry monkeys would fight over food, thirsty monkeys would fight over water, and, in general, any time more than one monkey in a group sought the same incentive simulta neously, a dispute would result and would be resolved through some form of aggression. However, the motivating force of competition for incentives began to be doubted when experiments like Southwick's on the reduction of space or the withholding of food failed to produce more than temporary increases in intra-group aggression. Indeed, food deprivation not only failed to increase aggression but in some cases actually resulted in decreased frequencies of aggression.

Studies of animals in the wild under conditions of extreme food deprivation likewise revealed that starving monkeys devoted almost all available energy to foraging, with little energy remaining for aggressive interaction. Furthermore, accumulating evidence from later studies of a variety of primate groups, for example, the study con ducted by Bernstein, indicates that one of the most potent stimuli for eliciting aggression is the introduction of an intruder into an organized group. Such introductions result in far more serious aggression than that produced in anyother types of experiments contrived to produce competition.

These studies of intruders suggest that adult members of the same species introduced to one another for the first time show considerable hostility because, in the absence of a social order, one must be established to control interanimal relationships. When a single new animal is introduced into an existing social organization, the newcomer meets even more serious aggression. Whereas in the first case aggression establishes a social order, in the second case resident animals mob the intruder, thereby initially excluding the new animal from the existing social unit. The simultaneous introduction of several animals lessens the effect, if only because the group divides its

笔 记 区

attention among the multiple targets. If, however, the several animals introduced to a group constitute their own social unit, each group may fight the opposing group as a unit; but, again, no individual is subjected to mass attack, and the very cohesion of the groups precludes prolonged individual combat. The submission of the defeated group, rather than unleashing unchecked aggression on the part of the victorious group, reduces both the intensity and frequency of further attack. Monkey groups therefore see to be organized primarily to maintain their established social order rather than to engage in hostilities perse.

17. The author of the passage is primarily concerned with
    (A) advancing a new methodology for changing a monkey' social behavior
    (B) comparing the methods of several research studies on aggression among monkeys
    (C) explaining the reasons for researchers' interest in monkeys' social behavior
    (D) discussing the development of investigators' theories about aggression among monkeys
    (E) examining the effects of competition on monkeys' social behavior

18. Which of the following best summarizes the findings reported in the passage about the effects of food deprivation on monkeys' behavior?
    (A) Food deprivation has no effect on aggression among monkeys.
    (B) Food deprivation increases aggression among monkeys because one of the most potent stimuli for eliciting aggression is the competition for incentives.
    (C) Food deprivation may increase long-term aggression among monkeys in a laboratory setting, but it produces only temporary increases among monkeys in the wild.
    (D) Food deprivation may temporarily increase aggression among monkeys, but it also leads to a decrease in conflict.
    (E) Food deprivation decreases the intensity but not the frequency of aggressive incidents among monkey.

19. According to the author, studies such as Southwick's had which of the following effects on investigators theories about monkeys' social behavior?
    (A) They suggested that existing theories about the role of aggression among monkeys did not fully account for the monkeys' ability to maintain an established social order.
    (B) They confirmed investigators' theories about monkeys' aggressive response to competition for food and water.
    (C) They confirmed investigators' beliefs about the motivation for continued aggression among monkeys in the same social group.
    (D) They disproved investigators' theory that the introduction of intruders in an

笔记区

organized monkey group elicits intragroup aggressive behavior.
(E) They cast doubt on investigators' theories that could account for observed patterns of aggression among monkeys.

20. The passage suggests that investigators of monkeys social behavior have been especially interested in aggressive behavior among monkeys because
(A) aggression is the most common social behavior among monkeys
(B) successful competition for incentives determines the social order in a monkey group
(C) situations that elicit aggressive behavior can be studied in a laboratory
(D) most monkeys are potentially aggressive, yet they live in social units that could not function without control of their aggressive impulses
(E) most monkeys are social, yet they frequently respond to newcomers entering existing social units by attacking them

21. It can be inferred from the passage that the establishment and preservation of social order among a group of monkeys is essential in order to
(A) keep the monkeys from straying and joining other groups
(B) control aggressive behavior among group members
(C) prevent the domination of that group by another
(D) protect individuals seeking to become members of that group from mass attack
(E) prevent aggressive competition for incentives between that group and another

22. The passage supplies information to answer which of the following questions?
(A) How does the reduction of space affect intragroup aggression among monkeys in an experimental setting?
(B) Do family units within a monkey social group compete with other family units for food?
(C) What are the mechanisms by which the social order of an established group of monkeys controls aggression within that group?
(D) How do monkeys engaged in aggression with other monkeys signal submission?
(E) Do monkeys of different species engage in aggression with each other over food?

23. Which of the following best describes the organization of the second paragraph?
(A) A hypothesis is explained and counter evidence is described.
(B) A theory is advanced and specific evidence supporting it is cited.
(C) Field observations are described and a conclusion about their significance is drawn.
(D) Two theories are explained and evidence supporting each of them is detailed.

笔 记 区

(E) An explanation of a general principle is stated and specific examples of its operation are given.

Analysis of prehistoric air trapped in tiny bubbles beneath the polar ice sheets and of the composition of ice surrounding those bubbles suggests a correlation between carbon dioxide levels in the Earth's atmosphere and global temperature over the last 160,000 years. Estimates of global temperature at the time air in the bubbles was trapped rely on measuring the relative abundances of hydrogen and its heavier isotope, deuterium, in the ice surrounding the bubbles. When global temperatures are relatively low, water containing deuterium tends to condense and precipitate before reaching the poles; thus, ice deposited at the poles when the global temperature was cooler contained relatively less deuterium than ice deposited at warmer global temperatures. Estimates of global temperature based on this information, combined with analysis of the carbon dioxide content of air trapped in ice deep beneath the polar surface, suggest that during periods of postglacial warming carbon dioxide in the Earth's atmosphere increased by approximately 40 percent.

24. In the passage, the author is primarily concerned with doing which of the following?

(A) Describing a new method of estimating decreases in global temperature that have occurred over the last 160,000 years

(B) Describing a method of analysis that provides information regarding the relation between the carbon dioxide content of the Earth's atmosphere and global temperature

(C) Presenting information that suggests that global temperature has increased over the last 160,000 years.

(D) Describing the kinds of information that can be gleaned from a careful analysis of the contents of sheets

(E) Demonstrating the difficulty of arriving at a firm conclusion regarding how increases in the amount of carbon dioxide in the Earth's atmosphere affect global temperature

25. It can be inferred from the passage that during periods of post glacial warming, which of the following occurred?

(A) The total volume of air trapped in bubbles beneath the polar ice sheets increased.

(B) The amount of deuterium in ice deposited at the poles increased.

(C) Carbon dioxide levels in the Earth atmosphere decreased.

(D) The amount of hydrogen in the Earth's atmosphere decreased relatively the amount of deuterium

(E) The rate at which ice was deposited at the poles increased

26. The author states that there is evidence to support which of the following assertions?

笔 记 区

(A) Estimates of global temperature that rely on measurements of deuterium in ice deposited at the poles are more reliable than those based on the amount of carbon dioxide contained in air bubbles beneath the polar surface.
(B) The amount of deuterium in the Earth's atmosphere tends to increase as global temperature decreases.
(C) Periods of post glacial warming are characterized by the presence of increased levels of carbon dioxide in the Earth's atmosphere.
(D) Increases in global temperature over the last 160,000 years are largely the result of increases in the ratio of deuterium to hydrogen in the Earth's atmosphere.
(E) Increases in global temperature over the last 160,000 years have been accompanied by decreases in the amount of deuterium in the ice deposited at the poles.

27. It can be inferred from the passage that the conclusion stated in the last sentence would need to be reevaluated if scientists discovered that which of the following were true?
(A) The amount of deuterium in ice deposited on the polar surface is significantly greater than the amount of deuterium in ice located deep beneath the polar surface.
(B) Both the air bubbles trapped deep beneath the polar surface and the ice surrounding them contain relatively low levels of deuterium.
(C) Air bubbles trapped deep beneath the polar surface and containing relatively high levels of carbon dioxide are surrounded by ice that contained relatively low levels of deuterium.
(D) The current level of carbon dioxide in the Earth's atmosphere exceeds the level of carbon dioxide in the prehistoric air trapped beneath the polar surface.
(E) Increases in the level of carbon dioxide in the Earth's atmosphere are accompanied by increases in the amount of deuterium in the ice deposited at the poles.

28. CUMBERSOME:
(A) likely to succeed
(B) reasonable to trust
(C) valuable to have
(D) easy to handle
(E) important to know

29. INDUCEMENT:
(A) reproof
(B) deterrent
(C) partiality

笔 记 区

(D) distinction
(E) consideration

30. STARTLE:
(A) appease
(B) lull
(C) reconcile
(D) dally
(E) slumber

31. ANOMALY:
(A) derivation from estimates
(B) conformity to norms
(C) return to origins
(D) adaptation to stresses
(E) repression of traits

32. RECIPROCATING:
(A) releasing slowly
(B) calculating approximately
(C) accepting provisionally
(D) moving unidirectionally
(E) mixing thoroughly

33. MOLLYCODDLE:
(A) talk boastfully
(B) flee swiftly
(C) treat harshly
(D) demand suddenly
(E) adjust temporarily

34. SURFEIT:
(A) affirmation
(B) compromise
(C) dexterity
(D) deficiency
(E) languor

35. SANGUINE:
(A) morose
(B) puzzled

笔 记 区

(C) gifted

(D) witty

(E) persistent

36. RETROSPECTIVE:

(A) irresolute

(B) hopeful

(C) unencumbered

(D) evanescent

(E) anticipatory

37. ENCOMIUM:

(A) biased evaluation

(B) polite response

(C) vague description

(D) harsh criticism

(E) sorrowful expression

38. FACTIONAL:

(A) excessive

(B) undistinguished

(C) disdainful

(D) disinterested

(E) disparate

SECTION 5

Time-30 minute 30 Questions

1. 1 $\frac{1}{2^1}+\frac{1}{2^2}+\frac{1}{2^3}$

r and s are integers, and $r<s$.

2. The number of odd integers between r and s The number of even integers between r and s

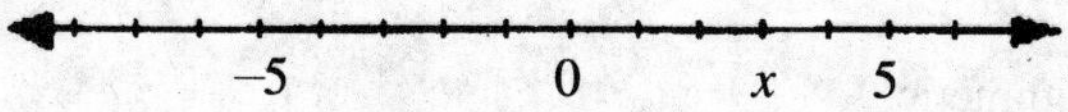

3. $x-y$ $x+y$

4. $10x-x$ 10

On a drawing done to scale, $\frac{1}{4}$ inch represents 5 feet.

5. The number of inches on the drawing that represents 150 feet 7.5

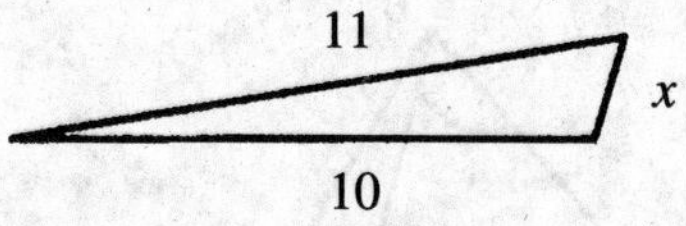

6. x 3

$y>0$

$x=3y$

7. 20 percent of x 50 percent of y

In a certain order of goods, $\frac{1}{3}$ of the items are shirts costing \$18 each and $\frac{2}{3}$ of the items are hats costing \$12 each.

8. The average (arithmetic mean) cost per item in the order	\$15

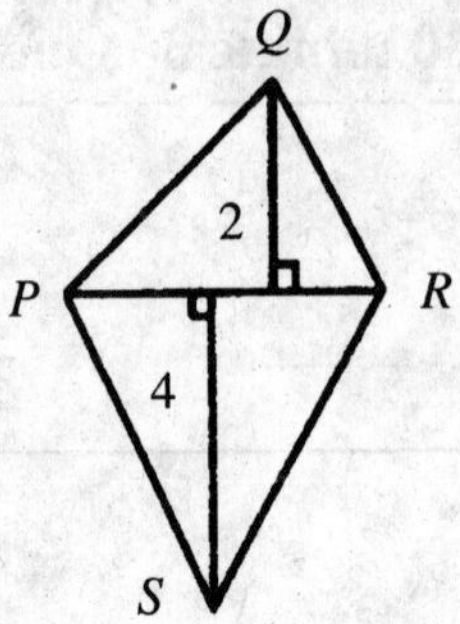

9. The area of triangular region *PRS*	Twice the area of triangular region *PQR*

$xy<0$

10. $x-y$	0
11. The average (arithmetic mean) of $\frac{10}{11}$ and $\frac{11}{10}$	1

$d>0$

12. The area of a circular region with diameter	The area of a square region with diagonal of length d
13. $\frac{(0.83)^6}{(0.83)^7}$	1

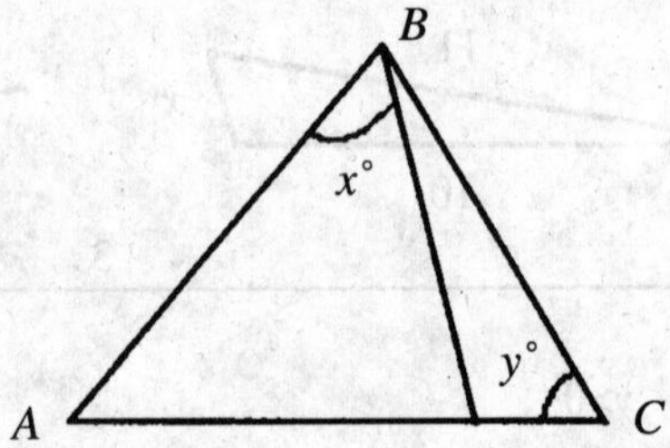

$AB=AC$

14. x	y

笔 记 区

15. $(2x+3y)^2$ $4x^2+6xy+9y^2$

TEMPERATURES IN DEGREES FAHRENHEIT RECORDED AT NOON ON THE FIRST FOUR DAYS OF CERTAIN MONTHS

Month	Temperatures
January	32,14,24,28
April	45,50,58,47
June	76,80,74,79
August	84,95,100,89
November	48,43,39,42

16. In a set of measurements, the range is defined as the greatest measurement minus the least measurement.
According to the table above, during the first four days of which month was the range of temperatures at noon the greatest?
(A) January
(B) April
(C) June
(D) August
(E) November

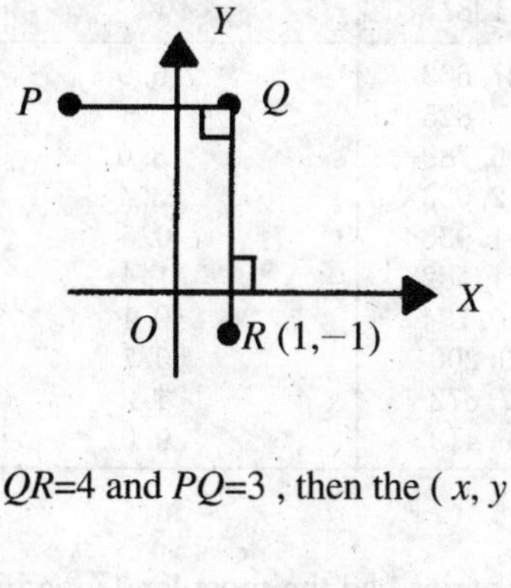

17. In the figure above, if $QR=4$ and $PQ=3$, then the (x, y) coordinates of point P are
(A) (−4, 4)
(B) (−3, 4)
(C) (−3, 3)
(D) (−2, 3)
(E) (−2, 4)

18. If $x^2=18$, then $|x|=$
(A) −9
(B) 9
(C) $2\sqrt{3}$

笔 记 区

(D) $-3\sqrt{2}$

(E) $3\sqrt{2}$

19. If $y-2x=-6$, then $8x-4y=$

(A) 24

(B) $\frac{3}{2}$

(C) 0

(D) $-\frac{3}{2}$

(E) −24

20. A car gets 22 miles per gallon using gasoline costing $1.10 per gallon. What is the approximate cost, in dollars, for driving the car x miles using this gasoline?

(A) $0.50x$

(B) $0.30x$

(C) $0.11x$

(D) $0.10x$

(E) $0.05x$

<u>Questions 21-25</u> refer to the following table.

POPULATION DATA FOR TEN SELECTED STATES IN 1980 AND 1987

State	Population (in thousands)		Percent Change in Population, 1980-1987	Population Per Square Mile in 1987
	1980	1987		
A	23, 668	27, 663	16. 9	177
B	17, 558	17, 825	1. 5	372
C	14, 229	16, 789	18. 0	64
D	9, 746	12, 023	23. 4	222
E	11, 864	11, 936	0. 6	266
F	11, 427	11, 582	1. 4	208
G	10, 798	10, 784	-0. 1	263
H	9, 262	9, 200	-0. 7	162
I	7, 365	7, 672	4. 2	1, 027
J	5, 882	6, 413	9. 0	131

21. Which of the following states had the most land area in 1987?

(A) A

(B) B

(C) C

(D) D

(E) E

22. In 1987 the average (arithmetic mean) population of the three most populous of the ten selected states was most nearly equal to

笔 记 区

(A) 18 million

(B) 19 million

(C) 20 million

(D) 21 million

(E) 22 million

23. If the land area of State J was the same in 1980 as it was in 1987, then the population square mile of State J in 1980 was most nearly equal to

(A) 140

(B) 130

(C) 120

(D) 110

(E) 100

24. If ranked from highest to lowest according to population, how many of the ten states changed in rank from 1980 to 1987?

(A) One

(B) Two

(C) Three

(D) Four

(E) Five

25. Of the following expressions, which represents the population per square mile of the region consisting of states B and E in 1987?

(A) $\dfrac{372+266}{2}$

(B) $\dfrac{17{,}825+11{,}936}{372+266}$

(C) $\dfrac{17{,}825}{372}+\dfrac{11{,}936}{266}$

(D) $\dfrac{372}{17{,}825}+\dfrac{266}{11{,}936}$

(E) $\dfrac{17{,}825+11{,}936}{\dfrac{17{,}825}{372}+\dfrac{11{,}936}{266}}$

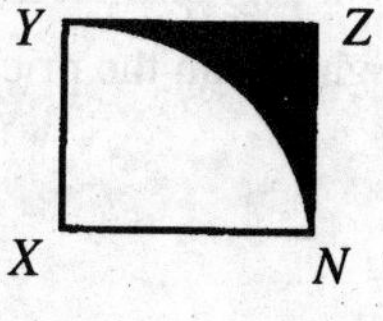

26. In the figure above, XYZW is a square with sides of length s. If YW is the arc of a circle with center X, which of the following is the area of the shaded region in terms of s?

(A) $\pi x^2-(\dfrac{S}{2})^2$

(B) $s^2-\pi s^2$

(C) $s^2-\frac{1}{4}\pi s^2$

(D) $4s-\pi s$

(E) $4s-\frac{1}{4}\pi s$

27. In a graduating class of 236 students, 142 took algebra and 121 took chemistry. What is the greatest number of students that could have taken both algebra and chemistry?

(A) 21

(B) 27

(C) 37

(D) 121

(E) 142

28. If one number is chosen at random from the first 1,000 positive integers, what is the probability that the number chosen is multiple of both 2 and 8?

(A) $\frac{1}{125}$

(B) $\frac{1}{8}$

(C) $\frac{1}{2}$

(D) $\frac{9}{16}$

(E) $\frac{5}{8}$

29. The price of product R is 20 percent higher than the price of product S, which in turn is 30 percent higher than the price of product T. The price of product R is what percent higher than the price of product T?

(A) 60%

(B) 56%

(C) 50%

(D) 44%

(E) 25%

$$\begin{array}{r} YX7 \\ +6Y \\ \hline Y7X \end{array}$$

30. In the sum above, if X and Y each denote one of the digits from 0 to 9, inclusive, then $X =$

(A) 9

(B) 5

(C) 3

(D) 1

(E) 0

笔 记 区

SECTION 6

Time-30 minute 38 Questions

1. If the theory is self-evidently true, as its proponents assert, then why does_____it still exist among well-informed people?
   (A) support for
   (B) excitement about
   (C) regret for
   (D) resignation about
   (E) opposition to

2. Although the_____of cases of measles has_____, researchers fear that eradication of the disease, once believed to be imminent, may not come soon.
   (A) occurrence...continued
   (B) incidence...declined
   (C) prediction...resumed
   (D) number...increased
   (E) study...begun

3. Nothing_____his irresponsibility better than his_____ delay in sending us the items he promised weeks ago.
   (A) justifies...conspicuous
   (B) characterizes...timely
   (C) epitomizes...unnecessary
   (D) reveals...conscientious
   (E) conceals...inexplicable

4. The author did not see the_____inherent in her scathing criticism of a writing style so similar to her own.
   (A) disinterest
   (B) incongruity
   (C) pessimism
   (D) compliment

笔 记 区

(E) symbolism

5. Whereas the Elizabethans struggled with the transition from medieval_____experience to modern individualism, we confront an electronic technology that seems likely to reverse the trend, rendering individualism obsolete and interdependence mandatory.
(A) literary
(B) intuitive
(C) corporate
(D) heroic
(E) spiritual

6. Our biological uniqueness requires that the effects of a substance must be verified by______experiments, even after thousands of tests of the effects of that substance on animals.
(A) controlled
(B) random
(C) replicated
(D) human
(E) evolutionary

7. Today water is more_______in landscape architecture than ever before, because technological advances have made it easy, in some instances even______to install water features in public places.
(A) conspicuous...prohibitive
(B) sporadic...effortless
(C) indispensable...intricate
(D) ubiquitous...obligatory
(E) controversial...unnecessary

Directions: In each of the following questions, a related pair of words or phrases is followed by five lettered pairs of words or phrases. Select the lettered pair that best expresses a relationship similar to that expressed in the original pair.

8. TERROR: FEAR::
(A) craving: desire
(B) inclination: liking
(C) sympathy: empathy
(D) urgency: lack
(E) alibi: excuse

9. FEED: HUNGER::

(A) reassure: uneasiness
(B) penetrate: inclusion
(C) abandon: desolation
(D) transfer: location
(E) fertilize: growth

10. PESTLE: GRIND::
(A) scissors: sharpen
(B) spice: flavor
(C) spoon: stir
(D) hammer: swing
(E) fan: rotate

11. DISSEMBLE: HONESTY::
(A) smile: amiability
(B) snub: politeness
(C) disagree: error
(D) flee: furtiveness
(E) elate: exuberance

12. SYNOPSIS: CONCISENESS::
(A) distillate: purity
(B) mutation: viability
(C) replication: precedence
(D) illusion: quickness
(E) icon: charity

13. MEDIATION : COMPROMISE::
(A) exclamation: remark
(B) approbation: acclaim
(C) election: legislation
(D) prosecution: conviction
(E) conclusion: evaluation

14. DEMOGRAPHY: POPULATION::
(A) agronomy: farm
(B) astronomy: planets
(C) chemistry: heat
(D) meteorology: weather
(E) genetics: adaptation

笔 记 区

15. EQUIVOCATION: TRUTH

(A) rhetoric: persuasion

(B) obfuscation: clarity

(C) metaphor: description

(D) repetition: boredom

(E) conciliation: appeasement

16. CRAVEN: ADMIRABLE::

(A) unruly: energetic

(B) listless: attractive

(C) deft: awkward

(D) trifling: amusing

(E) volatile: passionate

Bracken fern has been spreading from its woodland strongholds for centuries, but the rate of encroachment into open countryside has lately increased alarmingly throughout northern and western Britain. A tough competitor, bracken reduces the value of grazing land by crowding out other vegetation. The fern is itself poisonous to livestock, and also encourages proliferation of sheep ticks, which not only attack sheep but also transmit diseases. No less important to some people are bracken's effects on threatened habitats and on the use of uplands for recreational purposes, even though many appreciate its beauty. Biological controls may be the only economic solution. One potentially cheap and self-sustaining method of halting the spread of bracken is to introduce natural enemies of the plant. Initially unrestrained by predators of their own, foreign predators are likely to be able to multiply rapidly and overwhelm intended targets. Because bracken occurs throughout the world, there is plenty of scope for this approach. Two candidates, both moths from the Southern Hemisphere, are now being studied.

Of course, biological control agents can safely be released only if it can be verified that they feed solely on the target weed. The screening tests have so far been fraught with difficulties. The first large shipment of moths succumbed to a disease. Growing enough bracken indoors is difficult, and the moths do not readily exploit cut stems. These are common problems with rearing insects for biological control.

Other problems can be foreseen. Policymakers need to consider many factors and opinions such as the cost of control compared to existing methods, and the impact of the clearance of bracken on the landscape, wildlife, and vegetation. In fact, scientists already have much of the information needed to assess the impact of biological control of bracken, but it is spread among many individuals, organizations, and government bodies. The potential gains for the environment are likely to outweigh the losses because few plants, insects, mammals, and birds live associated only with bracken, and many would benefit from a return of other vegetation or from a more diverse mosaic of habitats. But legal consequences of attempts at biological control present a potential minefield. For example, many rural tenants still have the right of "estoyers" the right to cut bracken as bedding for livestock and uses. What would happen if they were deprived of these rights? Once a biological control agent is released, it is difficult to control its speed. What consideration is due landowners who do not want to control bracken? According to law, the release of the biological control agents must be authorized by the secretary of state for the environment. But Britain lacks the legal and administrative machinery to assemble evidence for and against release.

17. Which of the following best states the main idea of the passage?
(A) Studies suggest that biologicalcontrol of bracken will not be technically feasible.
(B) Although biological control appears to be the best solution to bracken infestation, careful assessment of the consequences is required.
(C) Environmentalists are hoping that laboratory technicians will find a way to raise large numbers of moths in captivity.
(D) Bracken is currently the best solution to the proliferation of nonnative moth species.
(E) Even after researchers discover the most economical method of pest control, the government has no authority to implement a control program.

18. According to the passage, which of the following can be inferred about sheep ticks?
(A) They increase where bracken spreads.
(B) They are dangerous only to sheep.
(C) They are especially adapted to woodland.
(D) They have no natural enemies.
(E) They cause disease among bracken.

19. The author cites all of the following as disadvantages of bracken encroachment EXCEPT:
(A) Bracken is poisonous to farm animals.
(B) Bracken inhibits the growth of valuable vegetation.
(C) Bracken indirectly helps spread certain diseases.
(D) Bracken is aesthetically objectionable.
(E) Bracken disturbs habitats that some people would like to protect.

20. The final paragraph can best be described as
(A) a summation of arguments presented in previous paragraphs
(B) the elimination of competing arguments to strengthen a single remaining conclusion
(C) an enumeration of advantages to biological control
(D) an expansion of the discussion from the particular example of bracken control to

the general problem of government regulation

(E) an overview of the variety of factors requiring further assessment

21. It can be inferred from the passage that it is advantageous to choose as the biological control agent a predator that is foreign to the targeted environment for which of the following reasons?

(A) Conservation groups prefer not to favor one native species over another.

(B) All local predators have already been overwhelmed by the target species.

(C) Local predators cannot be effectively screened since they already exist in the wild.

(D) There is little risk of an artificially introduced foreign predator multiplying out of control.

(E) Native predator species are generally limited by their own predators.

22. It can be inferred from the passage that the screening tests performed on the biological control agent are designed primarily to determine

(A) its effectiveness in eliminating the target species

(B) the response of local residents to its introduction

(C) the risk it poses to species other than the target

(D) its resistance to the stress of shipment

(E) the likelihood of its survival indoors

23. As it is discussed in the passage, the place of bracken within the forest habitat can best be described as

(A) rapidly expanding

(B) the subject of controversy

(C) well established

(D) circumscribed by numerous predators

(E) a significant nutrient source

Allen and Wolkowitz's research challenges the common claim that homework-waged labor performed at home for a company-is primarily a response to women workers' needs and preferences. By focusing on a limited geographical area in order to gather in-depth information, the authors have avoided the methodological pitfalls that have plagued earlier research on homework. Their findings disprove accepted notions about homeworkers: that they are unqualified for other jobs and that they use homework as a short-term strategy for dealing with child care.

The authors conclude that the persistence of homework cannot be explained by appeal to such notions, for, in fact, homeworkers do not differ sharply from other employed women. Most homeworkers would prefer to work outside the home but are constrained from doing so by lack of opportunity. In fact, homework is driven by employers' desires to minimize fixed costs: homeworkers receive no benefits and are paid less than regular employees.

24. The passage is primarily concerned with
(A) advocating a controversial theory
(B) presenting and challenging the results of a study
(C) describing a problem and proposing a solution
(D) discussing research that opposes a widely accepted belief
(E) comparing several explanations for the same phenomenon

25. According to the passage, which of the following has been generally believed about homework?
(A) The benefits of homework accrue primarily to employers rather than to homeworkers.
(B) Homework is prevalent predominantly in rural areas.
(C) Homework is primarily a response to the preferences of women workers.
(D) Few homeworkers rely on homework for the majority of their family income.
(E) Most homework is seasonal and part-time rather than full-time and year-round.

26. Allen and Wolkowitz's research suggests that each of the following is true of most homeworkers EXCEPT:
(A) They do not necessarily resort to homework as a strategy for dealing with child care.
(B) Their family situations are not unlike those of other employed women.
(C) They are as well qualified as women who work outside the home.
(D) They perform professional-level duties rather than manual tasks or piecework.
(E) They do not prefer homework to employment outside the home.

27. The passage suggests which of the following about previous research on homework?
(A) It was conducted primarily with women who did not have extensive household respon sibilities or care for small children at home.
(B) It was conducted with homeworkers and companies over a large geographical area.
(C) It indicated that women homeworkers had numerous opportunities to work outside the home.
(D) It indicated that homeworkers usually work for companies that are close to their homes.
(E) It indicated that homework was financially advantageous to large companies.

28. FLIPPANCY:
(A) temperance

(B) reliability
(C) seriousness
(D) inflexibility
(E) reticence

29. FACETIOUS:
(A) uncomplicated
(B) prideful
(C) earnest
(D) laconic
(E) forbearing

30. BUNGLE:
(A) bring off
(B) bail out:
(C) give in
(D) pull through
(E) put together

31. STODGY:
(A) nervous
(B) incisive
(C) exciting
(D) talkative
(E) happy

32. INIMITABLE:
(A) enviable
(B) reparable
(C) amicable
(D) unwieldy
(E) commonplace

33. SERE:
(A) lush
(B) obstinate
(C) immersed
(D) fortunate
(E) antiquated

34. VACUOUS:

(A) courteous
(B) exhilarated
(C) modest
(D) intelligent
(E) emergent

35. PEDESTRIAN:
(A) concise
(B) attractive
(C) mobile
(D) delicate
(E) imaginative

36. APPOSITE:
(A) disposable
(B) adjacent
(C) vicarious
(D) parallel
(E) extraneous

37. BOMBAST:
(A) kindness
(B) nonthreatening motion
(C) great effort
(D) down-to-earth language
(E) good-natured approval

38. LIMPID:
(A) unfading
(B) coarse
(C) elastic
(D) murky
(E) buoyant

笔 记 区

三、最新GRE
笔试模考练习题三

SECTION 1
Time-45 minutes

ISSUE TASK

Present your perspective on the issue you choose from the two topics below, using relevant reasons and /or examples to support your views

Topic 1:

"What most people consider 'normal' or 'natural' merely reflects the unexamined beliefs and preconceptions that this person received uncritically"

Topic 2:

"The purpose of education should be to create an academic environment that is separate from the outside world. This kind of environment is ideal because it allows students to focus on important ideas without being held back by practical concerns."

笔 记 区

SECTION 2

Time-30 minute

Argument task

Discuss how well reasoned you find this argument.

For the past five years, consumers in California have been willing to pay twice as much for oysters from the northeastern Atlantic Coast as for Gulf Coast oysters. This trend began shortly after harmful bacteria were found in a few raw Gulf Coast oysters. But scientists have now devised a process for killing the bacteria. Once consumers are made aware of the increased safety of Gulf Coast oysters, they are likely to be willing to pay as much for Gulf Coast as for northeastern Atlantic Coast oysters, and greater profits for Gulf Coast oyster producers will follow.

SECTION 3

Time-30 minute 38 Questions

1. While many Russian composers of the nineteenth century contributed to an emerging national style, other composers did not_____ idiomatic Russian musical elements, _____ instead the traditional musical vocabulary of Western European Romanticism.
(A) utilize...rejecting
(B) incorporate...preferring
(C) exclude...avoiding
(D) repudiate...expanding
(E) esteem...disdaining

2. Because the painter Albert Pinkham Ryder was obsessed with his_____perfection, he was rarely _____a painting, creating endless variations of a scene on one canvas, one on top of another.
(A) quest for...satisfied with
(B) insistence on...displeased with
(C) contempt for...disconcerted by
(D) alienation from...immersed in
(E) need for...concerned with

3. Objectively set standards can serve as a______for physicians, providing them ________unjustified malpractice claims.
(A) trial...evidence of
(B) model...experience with
(C) criterion...reasons for
(D) test...questions about
(E) safeguard...protection from

4. In spite of____reviews in the press, the production of her play was____almost certain oblivion by enthusiastic audiences whose acumen was greater than that of the critics.
(A) lukewarm...condemned to

笔 记 区

(B) scathing...exposed to
(C) lackluster...rescued from
(D) sensitive...reduced to
(E) admiring...insured against

5. The passions of love and pride are often found in the same individual, but having little in common, they mutually_____, not to say destroy, each other.
(A) reinforce
(B) annihilate
(C) enhance
(D) weaken
(E) embrace

6. The necessity of establishing discrete categories for observations frequently leads to attempts to make absolute_____when there are in reality only_____.
(A) analyses...hypotheses
(B) correlations...digressions
(C) distinctions...gradations
(D) complications...ambiguities
(E) conjectures...approximations

7. A unique clay disk found at the Minoan site of Phaistos is often____as the earliest example of printing by scholars who have defended its claim to this status despite equivalent claims put forward for other printing artifacts.
(A) questioned
(B) overlooked
(C) adduced
(D) conceded
(E) dismissed

8. EXEMPT: LIABILITY::
(A) flout: authority
(B) bestow: reward
(C) permit: request
(D) restrain: disorder
(E) pardon: penalty

9. FULL-BODIED: FLAVOR::
(A) penetrating: vision
(B) humorous: character
(C) salacious: language

笔 记 区

(D) nostalgic: feeling

(E) resonant: sound

10. LEGACY: PREDECESSOR::

(A) gift: donor

(B) gratuity: service

(C) contribution: charity

(D) receipt: customer

(E) loan: collector

11. HERO: ADMIRABLE::

(A) critic: capricious

(B) braggart: surly

(C) eccentric: unconventional

(D) anarchist: powerful

(E) enemy: immoral

12. GALVANIZE: STIMULATE::

(A) agitate: occlude

(B) incubate: humidify

(C) sterilize: separate

(D) irrigate: flush

(E) purify: amalgamate

13. MANIFEST: PERCEIVE::

(A) porous: tear

(B) renovated: improve

(C) doubtful: assess

(D) brittle: break

(E) elite: qualify

14. LOOSE: CONFINEMENT::

(A) forgive: injury

(B) promulgate: rule

(C) disabuse: misconception

(D) redress: allegation

(E) disengage: independence

15. BLANDISHMENT: COAX::

(A) prevarication: deceive

(B) reverie: dream

(C) persuasion: coerce
(D) enticement: impoverish
(E) explanation: mislead

16. CONVULSION: CONTRACTION::
(A) aggression: attack
(B) sulkiness: punishment
(C) persistence: acquiescence
(D) frenzy: emotion
(E) indifference: greeting

Much of the research on hallucinogenic drugs such as LSD has focused on the neurotransmitter serotonin, a chemical that when released from a presynaptic serotonin-secreting neuron causes the transmission of a nerve impulse across a synapse to an adjacent postsynaptic, or target, neuron. There are two major reasons for this emphasis. First, it was discovered early on that many of the major hallucinogens have a molecular structure similar to that of serotonin. In addition, animal studies of brain neurochemistry following administration of hallucinogens invariably reported changes in serotonin levels.

Early investigators correctly reasoned that the structural similarity to the serotonin molecule might imply that LSD's effects are brought about by an action on the neurotransmission of serotonin in the brain. Unfortunately, the level of technical expertise in the field of brain research was such that this hypothesis had to be tested on peripheral tissue (tissue outside the brain). Two different groups of scientists reported that LSD powerfully blockaded serotonin's action. Their conclusions were quickly challenged, however. We now know that the action of a drug at one site in the body does not necessarily correspond to the drug's action at another site, especially when one site is in the brain and the other is not.

By the 1960's, technical advances permitted the direct testing of the hypothesis that LSD and related hallucinogens act by directly suppressing the activity of serotonin-secreting neurons themselves — the so-called presynaptic hypothesis. Researchers reasoned that if the hllucinogenic drugs act by suppressing the activity of serotonin-secreting neurons, then drugs administered after these neurons had been destroyed should have no effect on behavior, because the system would already be maximally suppressed. Contrary to their expectations, neuron destruction enhanced the effect of LSD and related hallucinogens on behavior. Thus, hallucinogenic drugs apparently do not act directly on serotonin-secreting neurons.

However, these and other available data do support an alternative hypothesis, that LSD and related drugs act directly at receptor sites on serotonin target neurons (the postsynaptic hypothesis). The fact that LSD elicits "serotonin syndrome"—that is, causes the same kinds of behaviors as does the administration of serotonin—in animals whose brains are depleted of serotonin indicates that LSD acts directly on serotonin receptors, rather than indirectly through the release of stores of serotonin. The enhanced effect of LSD reported after serotonin depletion could be due to a proliferation of serotonin receptor sites on serotonin target neurons. This phenomenon often follows neuron destruction or neurotransmitter depletion; the increase in the number of receptor sites appears to be a compensatory response to decreased input. Significantly, this hypothesis is supported by data from a number of different laboratories.

17. According to the passage, which of the following is one of the primary factors that led researchers studying hallucinogenic drugs to focus on serotonin?
(A) The suppression of the activity of serotonin-secreting neurons by the administration of hallucinogens
(B) The observed similarities in the chemical structures of serotonin and hallucinogens
(C) The effects the administration of hallucinogens has on serotonin production in the human brain
(D) Serotonin-induced changes in the effects of hallucinogens on behavior
(E) Hallucinogen-induced changes in the effects of serotonin on behavior

18. It can be inferred that researchers abandoned the presynaptic hypothesis because
(A) a new and more attractive hypothesis was suggested
(B) no research was reported that supported the hypothesis
(C) research results provided evidence to counter the hypothesis
(D) the hypothesis was supported only by studies of animals and not by studies of human beings
(E) the level of technical expertise in the field of brain research did not permit adequate testing of the hypothesis

19. Which of the following best expresses the main idea of the passage?
(A) Research has suggested that the neurotransmitter serotonin is responsible for the effects of hallucinogenic drogs on the brain and on behavior.
(B) Researchers have spent an inadequate amount of time developing theories concerning the way in which the effects of hallucinogenic drugs occur.
(C) Research results strongly suggest that hallucinogenic drugs create their effects by acting on the serotonin receptor sites located on target neurons in the brain.
(D) Researchers have recently made valuable discoveries concerning the effects of depleting the amount of serotonin in the brain.
(E) Researchers have concluded that hallucinogenic drugs suppress the activity of serotonin-secreting neurons.

20. The research described in the passage is primarily concerned with answering which

of the following questions?

(A) How can researchers control the effects that LSD has on behavior?

(B) How are animal's reactions to LSD different from those of human beings?

(C) What triggers the effects that LSD has on human behavior?

(D) What technical advances would permit researchers to predict more accurately the effects of LSD on behavior?

(E) What relationship does the suppression of neuron activity have to the occurrence of "erotonin syndrome"

21. Which of the following best defines "erotonin syndrome" (line 29) as the term is used in the passage?

(A) The series of behaviors, usually associated with the administration of serotonin, that also occurs when LSD is administered to animals whose brains are depleted of serotonin

(B) The series of behaviors, usually associated with the administration of LSD, that also occurs when the amount of serotonin in the brain is reduced

(C) The maximal suppression of neuron activity that results from the destruction of serotonin-secreting neurons

(D) The release of stores of serotonin from serotonin-secreting neurons in the brain

(E) The proliferation of serotonin receptor sites that follows depletion of serotonin supplies in the brain

22. Which of the following best describes the organization of the argument that the author of the passage presents in the last two paragraphs?

(A) Two approaches to testing a hypothesis are described, and the greater merits of one approach are indicated.

(B) The assumptions underlying two hypotheses are outlined, and evidence for and against each hypothesis is discussed.

(C) A phenomenon is described, and hypotheses concerning its occurrence are considered and rejected.

(D) The reasoning behind a hypothesis is summarized, evidence supporting the hypothesis is presented, and research that counters the supporting evidence is described.

(E) A hypothesis is discussed, evidence undermining the hypothesis is revealed, and a further hypothesis based on the undermining evidence is explained

23. The author's attitude toward early researchers' reasoning concerning the implications of similarities in the structures of serotonin and LSD molecules can best be described as one of

(A) complete agreeement

(B) reluctant support

笔 记 区

(C) subtle condescension

(D) irreverent dismissal

(E) strong opposition

When literary periods are defined on the basis of men's writing, women's writing must be forcibly assimilated into an irrelevant grid: a Renaissance that is not a renaissance for women, a Romantic period in which women played very little part, a modernism with which women conflict. Simultaneously, the history of women's writing has been suppressed, leaving large, mysterious gaps in accounts of the development of various genres. Feminist criticism is beginning to correct this situation. Margaret Anne Doody, for example, suggests that during "the period between the death of Richardson and the appearance of the novels of Scott and Austen," which has "been regarded as a dead period." Late-eighteenth-century women writers actually developed "the paradigm for women's fiction of the nineteenth century—something hardly less than the paradigm of the nineteenth-century novel itself." Feminist critics have also pointed out that the twentieth-century writer Virginia Woolf belonged to a tradition other than modernism and that this tradition surfaces in her work precisely where criticism has hitherto found obscurities, evasions, implausibilities, and imperfections.

24. It can be inferred from the passage that the author views the division of literature into periods based on men's writing as an approach that

(A) makes distinctions among literary periods ambiguous

(B) is appropriate for evaluating only premodern literature

(C) was misunderstood until the advent of feminist criticism

(D) provides a valuable basis from which feminist criticism has evolved

(E) obscures women's contributions to literature

25. The passage suggests which of the following about Virginia Woolf's work?

Ⅰ. Nonfeminist criticism of it has been flawed.

Ⅱ. Critics have treated it as part of modernism.

Ⅲ. It is based on the work of late-eighteenth-century women writers.

(A) Ⅰ only

(B) Ⅱ only

(C) Ⅰ and Ⅱ only

(D) Ⅱ and Ⅲ only

(E) Ⅰ, Ⅱ and Ⅲ

26. The author quotes Doody most probably in order to illustrate

(A) a contribution that feminist criticism can make to literary criticism

(B) a modernist approach that conflicts with women's writing

(C) writing by a woman which had previously been ignored

(D) the hitherto overlooked significance of Scott's and Austen's novels

(E) a standard system of defining literary periods

27. The passage provides information that answers which of the following questions?

(A) In what tradition do feminist critics usually place Virginia Woolf?

(B) What are the main themes of women's fiction of the nineteenth century?

(C) What events motivated the feminist reinterpretation of literary history?

(D) How has the period between Richardson's death and Scott's and Ansten's novels traditionally been regarded by critics?

(E) How was the development of the nineteenth-century novel affected by women's fiction in the same century?

28. GROUNDED:

(A) attendant

(B) flawless

(C) effective

(D) aloft

(E) noteworthy

29. DISCHARGE:

(A) retreat

(B) hire

(C) insist

(D) circulate

(E) pause

30. INTERMITTENT:

(A) compatible

(B) constant

(C) neutral

(D) unadulterated

(E) indispensable

31. APT:

(A) exceptionally ornate

(B) patently absurd

(C) singularly destructive

(D) extremely inappropriate

(E) fundamentally insensitive

32. JUSTIFY:

笔 记 区

(A) misjudge
(B) ponder
(C) terminate
(D) argue against
(E) select from

33. TEDIOUS:
(A) intricate
(B) straightforward
(C) conspicuous
(D) entertaining
(E) prominent

34. INTEGRAL:
(A) profuse
(B) superfluous
(C) meritorious
(D) neutral
(E) displaced

35. COWED:
(A) unencumbered
(B) untired
(C) unversed
(D) unworried
(E) undaunted

36. CONCORD:
(A) continuance
(B) severance
(C) dissension
(D) complex relationship
(E) unrealistic hypothesis

37. FRIABLE:
(A) substantial
(B) inflexible
(C) easily contained
(D) slow to accelerate
(E) not easily crumbled

笔 记 区

38. DERACINATE:

(A) illuminate

(B) quench

(C) amplify

(D) polish

(E) plant

SECTION 4

Time-30 minute 30 Questions

The rent for each room at Hotel *X* was \$120 before it was increased 10 percent.

1. The rent for each room at Hotel *X* immediately after the increase	\$132

2. $\frac{1}{22.03-1.03}$	$\frac{1}{21}$

Train *X* traveled away from station A, and train *Y* traveled toward station A. The trains traveled toward each other on parallel tracks and passed each other at 10:30 A.M.

3. The number of minutes before 10:30 A.M.that train *X* traveled after leaving station A	The number of minutes after 10:30 A.M.that train *Y* before arriving at station A
4. The length of the hypotenuse of a right triangle with legs of lengths 3 and 4	The length of the hypotenuse of a right triangle with legs of lengths 2 and 5

The average (arithmetic mean)of the numbers 1, 2, 3, 4, and *n* is equal to 2.

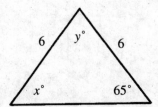

5. *n*	2

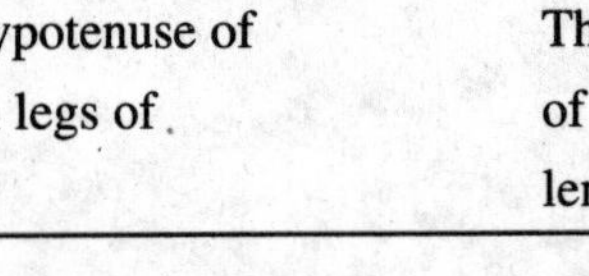

	Column A		Column B
6.	x		y
7.	$\frac{1}{m}+\frac{1}{n}$	$m \neq 0$, $n \neq 0$	$\frac{m+n}{m}$

Points P, Q, and R have rectangular coordinates(0,8), (4, 0), and (0,−3), respectively.

	Column A	Column B
8.	The perimeter of $\triangle PQR$	25

The result of multiplying $\frac{4}{5}z$ by $\frac{6}{7}$ is

	Column A	Column B
9.	z	1

$xyz<0$

$yz>0$

	Column A	Column B
10.	x	y
11.	$(0.01)^5$	$\frac{1}{10^{10}}$

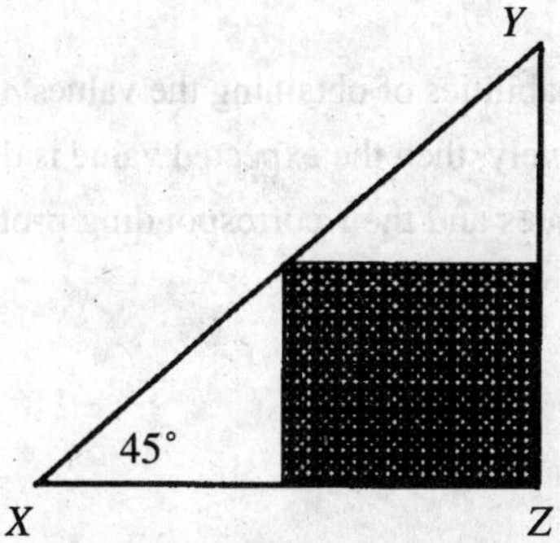

The shaded region is rectangular.

	Column A	Column B
12.	The perimeter of the shaded region	$XZ+YZ$
13.	3^{-5}	0

The sum of x and y is less than the product of x and y.

$y=\frac{1}{2}$

	Column A	Column B
14.	x	0

15. $\frac{10^7-10^6}{9}$ 100^3

16. If the range of the six measurements 140, 125, 180, 110, 165, and x is 80, which of the following could be the value of x ?

(A) 60

(B) 85

(C) 190

(D) 220

(E) 245

k	a_k	p_k
1	100	0.10
2	200	0. 25
3	300	0. 20
4	400	0. 25
5	500	0. 20

17. If in an experiment the probabilities of obtaining the values a_1, a_2, a_3, a_4, and a_5 are p_1, p_2, p_3, p_4, and p_5, respectively, then the expected value is defined as $a_1p_1+a_2p_2+a_3p_3+a_4p_4+a_5p_5$. For the values and their corresponding probabilities in the table above, what is the expected value?

(A) 350

(B) 320

(C) 300

(D) 270

(E) 250

18. If m is an integer, for what value of m is $3^m<100<3^{m+1}$?

(A) 0

(B) 1

(C) 2

(D) 3

(E) 4

19. A certain club is collecting money for a charity. A local company has agreed to contribute \$1 to the charity for every \$3 collected by the club. How much money

must the club collect in order for the total amount for the charity, including the company contribution, to equal $24,000?

(A) $18,000

(B) $16,000

(C) $15,000

(D) $12,000

(E) $10,000

20. A corner of a square tile is cut off, leaving the piece shown above. What is the area of this piece?

(A) 90 sq in

(B) 85 sq in

(C) 80 sq in

(D) 75 sq in

(E) 70 sq in

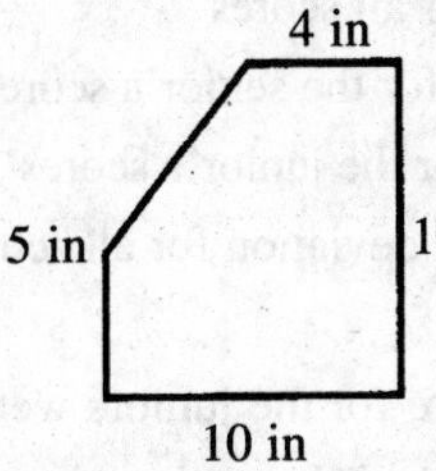

<u>Questions 21-25</u> refer to the following distribution.

TEST SCORES FOR A CLASS OF
8 JUNIORS AND 12 SENIORS

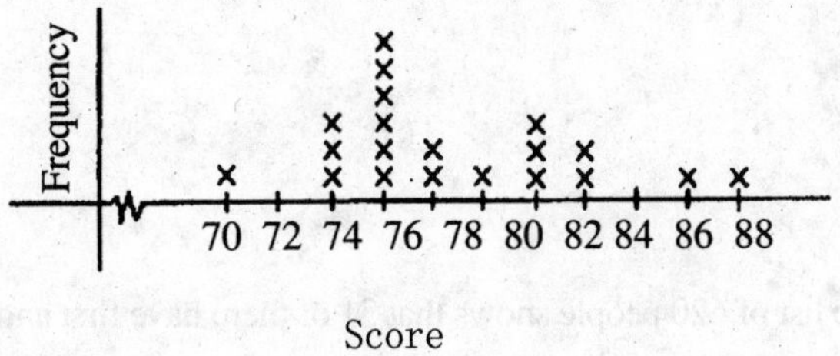

21. If 5 seniors have scores of 82 or above, how many juniors have scores below 82?

(A) 7

(B) 6

(C) 5

(D) 4

(E) 3

22. If 76 is the lowest passing score, what percent of the class <u>did</u> not get a passing score?

(A) 8%

(B) 10%

(C) 12%

(D) 20%

(E) 25%

笔 记 区

23. The median score for the class is
(A) 76
(B) 77
(C) 78
(D) 79
(E) 80

24. If 5 points were added to each score, which of the following would NOT be affected?
(A) The highest score
(B) The mean for all scores
(C) The median for the senior's scores
(D) The mode for the junior's scores
(E) The standard deviation for all scores

25. If the mean score for the juniors were known, which of the following could be calculated from the information given?
Ⅰ. The range of the scores for the seniors
Ⅱ. The median score for the juniors
Ⅲ. The mean score for the seniors
(A) None
(B) Ⅰ only
(C) Ⅲ only
(D) Ⅰ and Ⅱ
(E) Ⅱ and Ⅲ

26. A membership list of 620 people shows that 31 of them have first and last names that begin with the same letter. If a person is selected at random from the list, what is the probability that the person's first and last names do <u>not</u> begin with the same letter?
(A) 0.05
(B) 0.25
(C) 0.50
(D) 0.75
(E) 0.95

27. If p and r are prime numbers, which of the following must also be prime?
(A) pr
(B) $p + r$
(C) $pr + 1$
(D) $p^2 + r^2$
(E) None of the above

笔 记 区

28. For what ordered pair (x, y) on the graph of $y=\frac{1}{2}x-1$ does the x -coordinate equal the y -coordinate?

(A) $(-2,-2)$

(B) $(\frac{1}{2},\frac{1}{2})$

(C) $(1, -\frac{1}{2})$

(D) $(2, 1)$

(E) $(2, 2)$

29. David and Michael charged Mr. Jimenez \$3,000 to remodel his basement. To complete the project, David worked 4 days alone, Michael worked 1 day alone, and they worked 10 days together. If they each received the same amount of money for each day that they worked, how much of the \$3,000 did David receive?

(A) \$1,800

(B) \$1,750

(C) \$1,680

(D) \$1,575

(E) \$1,200

30. If x is positive and $6-x^2=$, $\frac{15}{16}$ then $\sqrt{x}=$

(A) $\frac{81}{16}$

(B) $\frac{9}{10}$

(C) $\frac{\sqrt{3}}{2}$

(D) $\frac{2}{3}$

(E) $\frac{3}{2}$

笔 记 区

SECTION 5

Time-30 minute 38 Questions

1. Punishment for violating moral rules is much more common than reward for following them; thus,______the rules goes almost______in society.
   (A) association with...undefended
   (B) adherence to...unnoticed
   (C) affiliation of...uncorrected
   (D) opposition to...unchecked
   (E) ignorance of...unresolved

2. Compassion is a great respecter of justice: we pity those who suffer______.
   (A) shamelessly
   (B) unwittingly
   (C) vicariously
   (D) intensively
   (E) undeservedly

3. No work illustrated his disdain for a systematic approach to research better than his dissertation, which was rejected primarily because his bibliography constituted, at best, ______survey of the major texts in his field.
   (A) an unimaginative
   (B) an orthodox
   (C) a meticulous
   (D) a comprehensive
   (E) a haphazard

4. In contrast to the______with which the acquisition of language by young children was once regarded, the process by which such learning occurs has now become the object of ______.
   (A) intensity...fascination
   (B) incuriosity...scrutiny
   (C) anxiety...criticism

(D) reverence...admiration

(E) impatience...training

5. The senator______remark that she is ambivalent about running for a second term is given the extremely______fund-raising activities of her campaign committee.

(A) disingenuous...reluctant

(B) futile...clandestine

(C) sincere...visible

(D) persuasive...apathetic

(E) straightforward...energetic

6. Until quite recently research on diabetes had, as a kind of holding action, attempted to refine the______of the disease, primarily because no preventive strategy seemed at all likely to be______.

(A) definition...necessary

(B) anticipation...acceptable

(C) understanding...costly

(D) treatment...practicable

(E) symptoms...feasible

7. Most plant species exhibit_______in their geographical distribution: often, a given species is found over a large geographical area, but individual populations within that range are widely_______.

(A) discontinuity...separated

(B) density...dispersed

(C) symmetry...observed

(D) uniformity...scattered

(E) concentration...adaptable

Directions: In each of the following questions, a related pair of words or phrases is followed by five lettered pairs of words or phrases. Select the lettered pair that best expresses a relationship similar to that expressed in the original pair.

8. FATIGUE: REST::

(A) gravity: weight

(B) friction: heat

(C) dehydration: water

(D) dizziness: vertigo

(E) radiation: light

9. RECYCLE: DISPOSAL::

笔 记 区

(A) recommend: insistence
(B) reciprocate: treatment
(C) rehabilitate: demolition
(D) attach: conquest
(E) offer: sale

10. DICTIONARY: ALPHABETICAL::
(A) map: contoured
(B) diary: anecdotal
(C) outline: detailed
(D) narrative: prosaic
(E) annals: chronological

11. ATTENUATE: THICKNESS::
(A) separate: substance
(B) ventilate: circulation
(C) vaccinate: immunity
(D) relocate: site
(E) debilitate: strength

12. SATIRE: RIDICULE::
(A) oration: enmity
(B) lullaby: dream
(C) parody: praise
(D) elegy: sorrow
(E) sonnet: remembrance

13. STOIC: PERTURB::
(A) perplexed: enlighten
(B) nondescript: neglect
(C) tranquil: pacify
(D) avaricious: satisfy
(E) daunting: bewilder

14. EXCULPATORY: ABSOLVE::
(A) motivational: stir
(B) conventional: resist
(C) rhetorical: speak
(D) pedantic: learn
(E) ponderous: choose

笔 记 区

15. MODERATE: INTENSITY::
(A) extenuate: seriousness
(B) separate: distance
(C) indulge: chaos
(D) commemorate: memorial
(E) disparage: animosity

16. JOLT: MOVE::
(A) possess: acquire
(B) arrive: remain
(C) check: stop
(D) spiral: turn
(E) rattle: hear

The origin of the theory that major geologic events may occur at regular intervals can be traced back not to a study of volcanism or plate tectonics but to an investigation of marine extinctions. In the early 1980's, scientists began to look closely at the question of how these extinctions occur. Two paleontologists, Raup and Sepkoski, compiled amaster list of marine species that died out duringthe past 268 million years and noted that there were brief periods during which many species disappeared at once. These mass extinctions occurred at surprisingly regular intervals.

Later studies revealed that extinctions of terrestrial reptiles and mammals also occurred periodically. These findings, combined with the research of Raup and Sepkoski, led scientists to hypothesize [the existence of some kind of cyclically recurring force powerful enough to affect living things profoundly. Speculation that so powerful a force might affect] gelogic events as well led geologists to search for evidence of periodicity in episodes of volcanism, seafloor spreading, and plate movement.

17. According to the passage, Raup and Sepkoski's research was concerned with
(A) learning more about the habitats of marine species
(B) studying plate tectonics and the occurrence of volcanism over the past 268 million years
(C) examining extinctions of marine species over the past 268 million years
(D) finding out whether a rhythmically recurring geologic force exists
(E) confirming previous evidence suggesting that extinction of terrestrial species occurred regularly

18. The author of the passage would most likely describe the findings of Roup and Sepkoski as
(A) plausible, because the findings supported the theories of previous researchers
(B) significant, because the findings were an impetus for subsequent research

(C) controversial, because the findings contradicted the theories of previous researchers

(D) questionable, because the authors were not working in their field of expertise

(E) definitive, because the findings confirmed the existence of a rhythmically recurring force

19. The author of the passage is primarily concerned with

(A) determining the dates of various geologic events

(B) defending the conclusions reached by Raup and Sepkoski

(C) establishing a link between the disciplines of paleontology and geology

(D) proving that mass extinctions of marine animals occur periodcally

(E) explaining how a theory concerning geologic events was formulated

20. The passage suggests which of the following about the "force" mentioned in lines 10 and 12?

(A) It is responsible for most of the major geologic events that have occurred.

(B) It is responsible for most of the marine extinctions that have occurred.

(C) Its recurrence is unlikely to be able to be predicted by scientists.

(D) Its existence was not seriously considered by scientists before Raup and Sepkoski did their research.

(E) Its existence was confirmed by the research of Raup and Sepkoski.

A recent history of the Chicago meat-packing industry and its workers examines how the industry grew from its appearance in the 1830's through the early 1890's. Meat-packers, the author argues, had good wages, working conditions, and prospects for advancement within the packinghouses, and did not cooperate with labor agitators since labor relations were so harmonious. Because the history maintains that conditions were above standard for the era, the frequency of labor disputes, especially in the mid-1880's, is not accounted for. The work ignores the fact that the 1880's were crucial years in American labor history, and that the packinghouse workers' efforts were part of the national movement for labor reform.

In fact, other historical sources for the late nine-teenth century record deteriorating housing and high disease and infant mortality rates in the industrial community, due to low wages and unhealthy working conditions. Additional data from the University of Chicago suggest that the packinghouses were dangerous places to work. The government investigation commissioned by President Theodore Roosevelt which eventually led to the adoption of the 1906 Meat Inspection Act found the packinghouses unsanitary, while social workers observed that most of the workers were poorly paid and overworked.

The history may be too optimistic because most of its data date from the 1880's at the latest, and the information provided from that decade is insufficiently analyzed.

Conditions actually declined in the 1880's, and continued to decline after the 1880's, due to a reorganization of the packing process and a massive influx of unskilled workers. The deterioration in worker status, partly a result of the new availability of unskilled and hence cheap labor, is not discussed. Though a detailed account of work in the packing-houses is attempted, the author fails to distinguish between the wages and conditions for skilled workers and for those unskilled laborers who comprised the majority of the industry's workers from the 1880's on. While conditions for the former were arguably tolerable due to the strategic importance of skilled workers in the complicated slaughtering, cutting, and packing process (though worker complaints about the rate and conditions of work were frequent), pay and conditions for the latter were wretched.

The author's misinterpretation of the origins of the feelings the meat-packers had for their industrial neighborhood may account for the history's faultygeneralizations. The pride and contentment the author remarks upon were, arguably, less the products of the industrial world of the packers—the giant yards and the intricate plants—than of the unity and vibrance of the ethnic cultures that formed a viable community on Chicago's South Side. Indeed, the strength of this community succeeded in generating a social movement that effectively confronted the problems of the industry that provided its livelihood.

21.The passage is primarily concerned with discussing

(A) how historians ought to explain the origins of the conditions in the Chicago meat-packing industry

(B) why it is difficult to determine the actual nature of the conditions in the Chicago meat-packing industry

(C) why a particular account of the conditions in the Chicago meat-packing industry is inaccurate

(D) what ought to be included in any account of the Chicago meat-packers' role in the national labor movement

(E) what data are most relevant for an accurate account of the relations between Chicago meat-packers and local labor agitators

22. The author of the passage mentions all of the following as describing negative conditions in the meat-packing industry EXCEPT

(A) data from the University of Chicago

(B) a recent history of the meat-packing industry

(C) social workers

(D) historical sources for the late nineteenth century

(E) government records

23. The author of the passage mentions the "social movement" (line 36) generated by

笔 记 区

Chicago's South Side community primarily in order to

(A) inform the reader of events that occurred in the meat-packing industry after the period of time covered by the history

(B) suggest the history's limitations by pointing out a situation that the history failed to explain adequately

(C) salvage the history's point of view by suggesting that there were positive developments in the meat-packing industry due to worker unity

(D) introduce a new issue designed to elaborate on the good relationship between the meat-packers and Chicago's ethnic communities

(E) suggest that the history should have focused more on the general issue of the relationship between labor movements and healthy industrial communities

24. According to the passage, the working conditions of skilled workers in the meat-packing industry during the 1880's were influenced by

(A) the workers' determined complaints about the rate and conditions of their work

(B) the efforts of social workers to improve sanitation in the packinghouses

(C) the workers' ability to perform the industry's complex tasks

(D) improvements in the industry's packing process that occurred in the 1880's

(E) opportunities for job advancement due to the filling of less desirable positions by increasing numbers of unskilled workers

25. The author of the passage uses the second paragraph to

(A) summarize the main point of the history discussed in the passage

(B) explain why the history discussed in the passage has been disparaged by critics

(C) evaluate the findings of recent studies that undermine the premises of the history discussed in the passage

(D) introduce a hypothesis that will be discussed in detail later in the passage

(E) present evidence that is intended to refute the argument of the history discussed in the passage

26. The tone of the author of the passage in discussing the meat-packer community on Chicago's South Side can best be described as one of

(A) appreciation of the community's ability to cope with difficult conditions

(B) admiration for the community's refusal to cooperate with labor agitators

(C) indignation at the kinds of social conditions the community faced

(D) annoyance at the community's inability to abolish discrimination in the meat-packing industry

(E) concern that the meat-packers' feelings for their community have not been documented

27. The information in the passage suggests that the author of the history discussed in

笔 记 区

the passage made which of the following errors?

(A) Failing to recognize the effect of the diversity of the South Side community on the meat-packers' efforts to reform the industry

(B) Attributing good working conditions in the meat-packing industry to the efforts of labor agitators

(C) Overemphasizing the importance of the availability of unskilled labor as an influence on conditions in the meat packing industry

(D) Interpreting the meat-packers' feelings for their community as appreciation of their industry

(E) Failing to observe the pride and contentment felt by the meat-packers

28. CELEBRITY:

(A) eccentricity

(B) informality

(C) obscurity

(D) aloofness

(E) nonchalance

29. CHRONIC:

(A) imminent

(B) asynchronous

(C) sequential

(D) sporadic

(E) spontaneous

30. ACCUMULATION:

(A) severance

(B) dissipation

(C) reciprocity

(D) absolution

(E) remuneration

31. CALCIFICATION:

(A) forgetfulness

(B) abundance

(C) streamlining

(D) clairvoyance

(E) flexibility

32. MIGRATORY:

笔 记 区

(A) speculative
(B) transitory
(C) sedentary
(D) kinetic
(E) convergent

33. CIVILITY:
(A) impassivity
(B) rudeness
(C) indiscretion
(D) dubiety
(E) indolence

34. VARIANCE:
(A) contingency
(B) congruity
(C) encumbrance
(D) usefulness
(E) distinctness

35. GENIAL:
(A) dyspeptic
(B) ceremonious
(C) wistful
(D) ravishing
(E) variable

36. DIURNAL:
(A) predictable
(B) ephemeral
(C) primitive
(D) nocturnal
(E) vestigial

37. APOLOGIST:
(A) accompanist
(B) protagonist
(C) supplicant
(D) critic
(E) conspirator

38. VIRULENT:

(A) auspicious

(B) polite

(C) salubrious

(D) vanquished

(E) intermittent

笔 记 区

SECTION 6

Time-30 minute 30 Questions

1. $\frac{2}{3}$ | $\frac{5}{6}$

$r = 7$
$s = -7$

2. $2r-2s+r^2$ | $2s-2r+s^2$

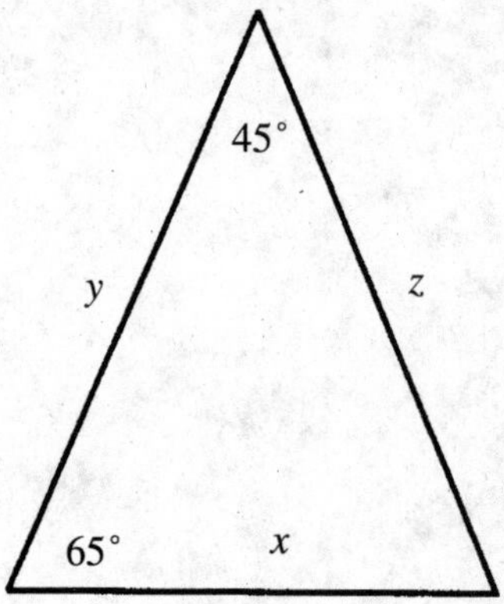

3. y | z

$0.1234 < n < 0.1245$

4. The thousandths digit of n | 4

5. The perimeter of a square with side of length 4 x | Four times the perimeter of a square with side of length x

$m-n=0$
$mn \neq 0$

6. $\frac{m}{m+n}$ | $\frac{1}{3}$

$10^x = 125y$

7. x y

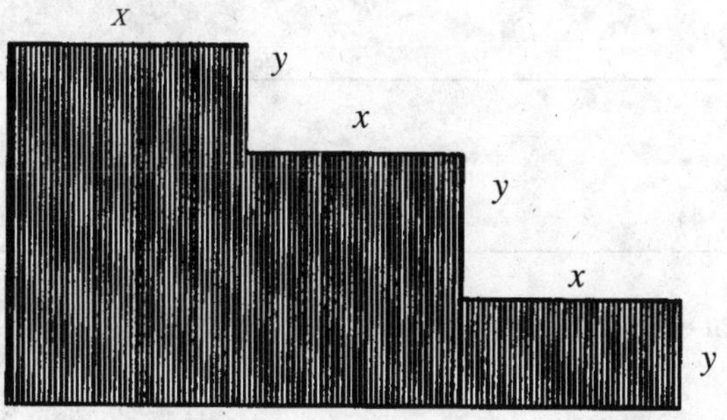

In the figure, all intersecting segments meet at right angles.

8. The area of the shaded region 6 xy

A total of 600 tickets to a concert were sold at prices ranging from \$10 to \$50 each.

9. The average (arithmetic mean) price per ticket \$30

10. $\frac{6}{\sqrt{3}}$ $2\sqrt{3}$

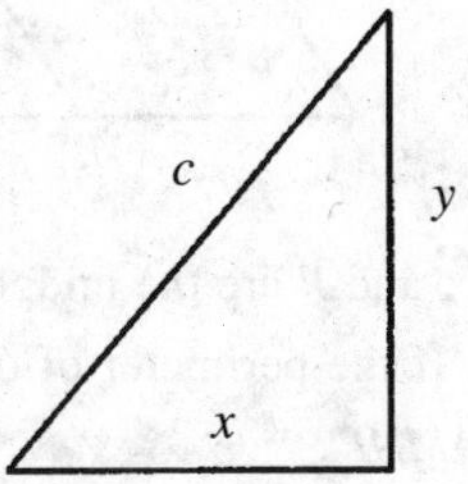

$xy = 12$

Column A Column B

C 5

11. C 5

A light-year is the distance that light travels in one year, or approximately 9.5×10^{12} kilometers. A certain star is 2.4×10^{15} kilometers away from the Sun.

12. The number of light-years that the star is away from the Sun 1,000

笔记区

E is the sum of the first 40 positive even integers.

K is the sum of the first 40 positive odd integers.

13.	E−K	40

$x = y$

14.	$5(y-4)$	$4(x-5)$

The probability that even t *R* will occur is 0.38.

15. The probability that events *R* and *W* will both occur	0.40

16. For a certain telephone company, it is projected that next year 2 out of every 3 new telephone numbers will be assigned to cellular telephones. If the company projects that a total of 1,200,000 new telephone numbers will be assigned next year, how many of these numbers are projected to be assigned to cellular telephones?
(A) 800,000
(B) 600,000
(C) 400,000
(D) 360,000
(E) 240,000

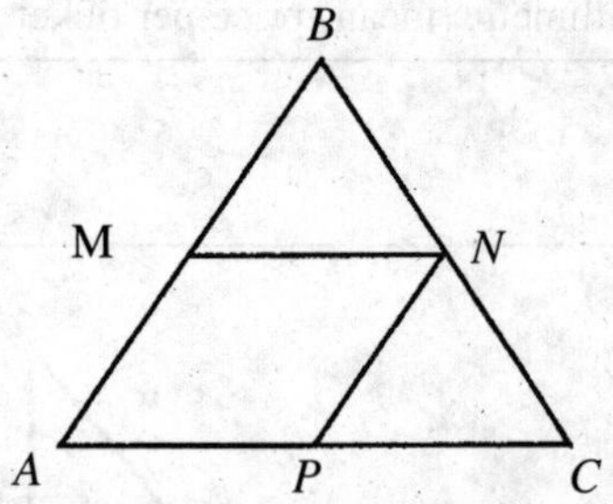

17. In the figure above, *M*, *N* , and *P* are the midpoints on the respective sides of equilateral triangle *ABC* . If the perimeter of triangle *ABC* is 24, what is the perimeter of quadrilateral *AMNP*?
(A) 8
(B) 16
(C) 32
(D) 48
(E) 64

18. Of the 500 delegates attending a convention, 200 are Republicans and the rest are Democrats. One hundred of the delegates are vegetarians and, of those who are not vegetarians, 270 are Democrats. How many of the vegetarian delegates are Republicans?
(A) 30
(B) 40
(C) 50

笔 记 区

(D) 60

(E) 70

19. If $3x=(x+2)(x-2)$, then x could be

(A) 2

(B) 1

(C) $\frac{1}{4}$

(D) -1

(E) -4

20. Art, Bob, and Carmen share a prize of \$400. If Art receives twice as much as Bob, and if Bob receives $\frac{1}{2}$ as much as Carmen, how much does Carmen receive?

(A) \$20

(B) \$40

(C) \$80

(D) \$140

(E) \$160

<u>Questions 21-25</u> refer to the following graph.

RIVER LEVELS OVER A SEVEN-DAY PERIOD

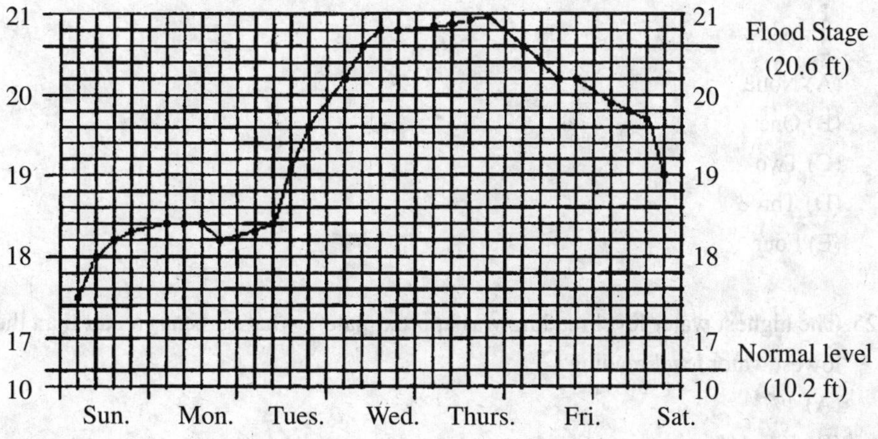

Note: Drawn to scale:

Water level readings taken at the same spot of the river each day at 7:00 and 11:00 in the morning, at 3:00 in the afternoon. and at 7:00 in the evening. respectively

21. Approximately how many feet from flood stage was the water level at 11:00 in the morning on Tuesday?

(A) 1.2

(B) 1.6

(C) 2.2

(D) 2.6

(E) 3.2

22. Which reading indicated the greatest rise in water level from the previous reading?

(A) Sunday at 11:00 in the morning

(B) Tuesday at 3:00 in the afternoon

(C) Tuesday at 7:00 in the evening

(D) Wednesday at 7:00 in the morning

(E) Thursday at 7:00 in the evening

23. Approximately what was the average rise in water level per hour from the last reading on Tuesday to the first reading on Wednesday?

(A) 0.05 feet

(B) 0.10 feet

(C) 0.15 feet

(D) 0.20 feet

(E) 0.25 feet

24. For how many successive pairs of readings was there a drop in water level of at least $\frac{1}{2}$ foot.

(A) None

(B) One

(C) Two

(D) Three

(E) Four

25. The highest water level reading was approximately what percent greater than the lowest water level reading?

(A) 4%

(B) 13%

(C) 16%

(D) 20%

(E) 24%

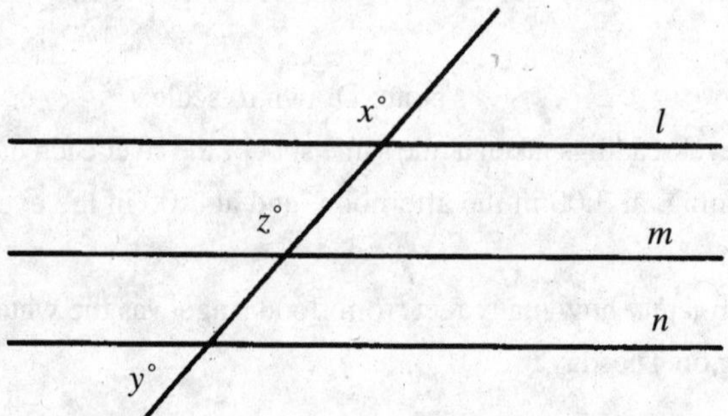

笔 记 区

26. In the figure above, if lines *l*, *m*, and *n* are parallel and $z=x+60$, what is the value of $x+y+z$?

(A) 120

(B) 150

(C) 180

(D) 210

(E) 240

27. The average (arithmetic mean) of 6 numbers is 49. How much greater would the average of the 7 numbers consisting of the original 6 numbers and the number 112 be than the average of the original 6 numbers?

(A) 9

(B) 31.5

(C) 55

(D) 63

(E) 80.5

28. According to a newspaper article about employment in Country *J*, 30.2 million workers, or 20.9 percent of the labor force of Country *J*, were union members. Which of the following equals the number of workers in millions in the labor force of Country *J*?

(A) (30,2) (20.9)

(B) (30.2) (0.209)

(C) $\frac{20.9}{0.302}$

(D) $\frac{30.2}{20.9}$

(E) $\frac{30.2}{0.209}$

29. If $x=\frac{y}{7}$, $z=\frac{x}{y}$, and $y \neq 0$, what is the value of $(z-1)^2$?

(A) $\frac{1}{49}$

(B) $\frac{36}{49}$

(C) $\frac{8}{7}$

(D) $\frac{64}{49}$

(E) $\frac{36}{7}$

笔 记 区

30. Which of the following CANNOT be expressed as the product of exactly 2 consecutive integers?

(A) (2) (3) (7)

(B) (2) (3) (7) (11)

(C) (2) (5^2) (13)

(D) (2^2) (3) (5) (7)

(E) (3^2) (11) (13)

笔 记 区

四、最新GRE
笔试模考练习题四

SECTION 1
Time-45 minutes

ISSUE TASK

Present your perspective on the issue you choose from the two topics below, using relevant reasons and /or examples to support your views

Topic 1:

The true strength of a country is best demonstrated by the willingness of its government to tolerate challenges from its own citizens.

SECTION 2

Time-30 minute

Argument task

Discuss how well reasoned you find this argument.

The Department of Education in the state of Attra recommends that high school students be assigned homework every day. Yet a recent statewide survey of high school math and science teachers calls the usefulness of daily homework into question. In the district of Sanlee, 86 percent of the teachers reported assigning homework three to five times a week, whereas in the district of Marlee, less than 25 percent of the teachers reported assigning homework three to five times a week. Yet the students in Marlee earn better grades overall and are less likely to be required to repeat a year of school than are the students in Sanlee. Therefore, all teachers in our high schools should assign homework no more than twice a week, if at all.

SECTION 3

Time-30 minute 38 Questions

1. There is hardly a generalization that can be made about people's social behavior and the values informing it that cannot be ______ from one or another point of view, or even ______ as simplistic or vapid.
(A) accepted...praised
(B) intuited...exposed
(C) harangued...retracted
(D) defended...glorified
(E) challenged...dismissed

2. Although any destruction of vitamins caused by food irradiation could be ______ the use of diet supplements, there may be no protection from carcinogens that some fear might be introduced into foods by the process.
(A) counterbalanced by
(B) attributed to
(C) inferred from
(D) augmented with
(E) stimulated by

3. Though he refused any responsibility for the failure of the negotiations, Stevenson had no right to ______ himself: it was his ______ that had caused the debacle.
(A) blame...skill
(B) congratulate...modesty
(C) berate...largesse
(D) accuse...obstinacy
(E) absolve...acrimony

4. The prevailing union of passionate interest in detailed facts with equal devotion to abstract ______ is a hallmark of our present society; in the past this union appeared, at best, ______ and as if by chance.
(A) data...extensively

(B) philosophy...cyclically
(C) generalization...sporadically
(D) evaluation...opportunely
(E) intuition....selectively

5. A century ago the physician's word was ______ to doubt it was considered almost sacrilegious
(A) inevitable
(B) intractable
(C) incontrovertible
(D) objective
(E) respectable

6. So much of modern fiction in the United States is autobiographical, and so much of the autobiography fictionalized, that the ______ sometimes seem largely ______.
(A) authors...ignored
(B) needs...unrecognized
(C) genres...interchangeable
(D) intentions...misunderstood
(E) misapprehensions...uncorrected

7. Robin's words were not without emotion: they retained their level tone only by a careful _______ imminent extremes.
(A) equipoise between
(B) embrace of
(C) oscillation between
(D) limitation to
(E) subjection to

8. OIL : LUBRICATE::
(A) preservative : desiccate
(B) wine : ferment
(C) honey : pollinate
(D) antiseptic : disinfect
(E) soil : fertilize

9. CONSTRUCT : REMODEL::
(A) exhibit : perform
(B) compose : edit
(C) demolish : repair

笔 记 区

(D) quantify : estimate
(E) predict : assess

10. SPOKE : HUB::
(A) radius : center
(B) parabola : equation
(C) line : point
(D) vector : direction
(E) slope : change

11. ILLUSTRATE : PICTURES::
(A) particularize : details
(B) abridge : texts
(C) parse : sentences
(D) regularize : inconsistencies
(E) economize: words

12. PANTRY : FOOD::
(A) museum : replicas
(B) ship : cargo
(C) office : business
(D) armory : weapons
(E) warehouse : storage

13. MIRTH : LAUGHTER::
(A) uncertainty : nod
(B) approval : applause
(C) danger : alarm
(D) labor : sweat
(E) love : respect

14. ABRADED : FRICTION::
(A) refined : combustion
(B) attenuated : coagulation
(C) diluted : immersion
(D) strengthened : compression
(E) desiccated : dehydration

15. PARSIMONY : MISER::
(A) temerity : despot
(B) belligerence: traitor

笔 记 区

(C) remorse : delinquent
(D) equanimity : guardian
(E) rebelliousness: insurgent

16. NITPICK : CRITICIZE::
(A) mock : imitate
(B) complain : argue
(C) interrogate : probe
(D) fret : vex
(E) cavil : object

Directions: Each passage in this group is followed by questions based on its content. After reading a passage, choose the best answer to each question. Answer all questions following a passage on the basis of what is stated or implied in that passage.

(This passage is from a book published in 1960.)

When we consider great painters of the past, the study of art and the study of illusion cannot always be separated. By illusion I mean those contrivances of color, line, shape, and so forth that lead us to see marks on a flat surface as depicting three-dimensional objects in space. I must emphasize that I am not making a plea, disguised or otherwise, for the exercise of illusionist tricks in painting today, although I am, in fact, rather critical of certain theories of non representational art. But to argue over these theories would be to miss the point. That the discoveries and effects of representation that were the pride of earlier artists have become trivial today I would not deny for a moment. Yet I believe that we are in real danger of losing contact with past masters if we accept the fashionable doctrine that such matters never had anything to do with art. The very reason why the representation of nature can now be considered something commonplace should be of the greatest interest to art historians. Never before has there been an age when the visual image was so cheap in every sense of the word. We are surrounded and assailed by posters and advertisements, comics and magazine illustrations. We see aspects of reality represented on television, postage stamps, and food packages. Painting is taught in school and practiced as a pastime, and many modest amateurs have mastered tricks that would have looked like sheer magic to the fourteenth-century painter Giotto. Even the crude colored renderings on a cereal box might have made Giottoís contemporaries gasp. Perhaps there are people who conclude from this that the cereal box is superior to a Giotto; I do not. But I think that the victory and vulgarization of representational skills create a problem for both art historians and critics.

In this connection it is instructive to remember the Greek saying that to marvel is the beginning of knowledge and if we cease to marvel we may be in danger of ceasing to know. I believe we must restore our sense of wonder at the capacity to conjure up by forms, lines, shades, or colors those mysterious phantoms of visual reality we call ìpictures.î Even comics and advertisements, rightly viewed, provide food for thought. Just as the study of poetry remains incomplete without an awareness of the language of prose, so, I believe, the study of art will be increasingly supplemented by inquiry into the ìlinguisticsî of the [visual image. The way the language of art refers to the visible world is both so obvious and so mysterious that it is still largely unknown except to artists who use it as we use all language-without needing to know its grammar and semantics.]

17. The author of the passage explicitly, <u>disagrees</u> with which of the following statements?
(A) In modern society even nonartists can master techniques that great artists of the fourteenth century did not employ.
(B) The ability to represent a three-dimensional object on a flat surface has nothing to do with art.
(C) In modern society the victory of representational skills has created a problem for art critics.
(D) The way that artists are able to represent the visible world is an area that needs a great deal more study before it can be fully understood.
(E) Modern painters do not frequently make use of illusionist tricks in their work.

18. The author suggests which of the following about art historians?
(A) They do not believe that illusionist tricks have become trivial.
(B) They generally spend little time studying contemporary artists.
(C) They have not given enough consideration to how the representation of nature has become commonplace.
(D) They generally tend to argue about theories rather than address substantive issues.
(E) They are less likely than art critics to study comics or advertisements.

19. Which of the following best states the author's attitude toward comics, as expressed in the passage?
(A) They constitute an innovative art form.
(B) They can be a worthwhile subject for study.
(C) They are critically important to an understanding of modem art.
(D) Their visual structure is more complex than that of medieval art.
(E) They can be understood best if they are examined in conjunction with advertisements.

20. The author's statement regarding how artists use the language of art (lines 30-33)

笔 记 区

implies that

(A) Artists are better equipped than are art historians to provide detailed evaluations of other artistsí work

(B) Many artists have an unusually quick, intuitive understanding of language

(C) Artists can produce works of art even if they cannot analyze their methods of doing so

(D) Artists of the past, such as Giotto, were better educated about artistic issues than were artists of the authorís time

(E) Most artists probably consider the processes involved in their work to be closely akin to those involved in writing poetry

21. The passage asserts which of the following about commercial art?

(A) There are many examples of commercial art whose artistic merit is equal to that of great works of art of the past.

(B) Commercial art is heavily influenced by whatever doctrines are fashionable in the serious art world of the time.

(C) The line between commercial art and great art lies primarily in how an image is used, not in the motivation for its creation.

(D) The level of technical skill required to produce representational imagery in commercial art and in other kinds of art cannot be compared.

(E) The pervasiveness of contemporary commercial art has led art historians to undervalue representational skills.

22. Which of the following can be inferred from the passage, about the adherents of "certain theories of nonrepresentational art" (line 6)?

(A) They consider the use of illusion to be inappropriate in contemporary art.

(B) They do not agree that marks on a flat surface can ever satisfactorily convey the illusion of three-dimensional space.

(C) They do not discuss important works of art created in the past.

(D) They do not think that the representation of nature was ever the primary goal of past painters.

(E) They concern themselves more with types of art such as advertisements and magazine illustrations than with traditional art.

23. It can be inferred from the passage that someone who wanted to analyze the "grammar and semantics"(line 32-33) of the language of art would most appropriately comment on which of the following?

(A) The relationship between the drawings in a comic strip and the accompanying text

(B) The amount of detail that can be included in a tiny illustration on a postage stamp

(C) The sociological implications of the images chosen to advertise a particular

笔 记 区

product

(D) The degree to which various colors used in different versions of the same poster would attract the attention of passersby

(E) The particular juxtaposition of shapes in an illustration that makes one shape look as though it were behind another

The 1973 Endangered Species Act made into legal policy the concept that endangered species of wildlife are precious as part of a natural ecosystem. The nearly unanimous passage of this act in the United States Congress, reflecting the rising national popularity of environmentalism, masked a bitter debate. Affected industries clung to the former wildlife policy of valuing individual species according to their economic usefulness. They fought to minimize the law's impact by limiting definitions of key terms, but they lost on nearly every issue. The act defined "wildlife" as almost all kinds of animals—from large mammals to invertebrates-and plants. "Taking" wildlife was defined broadly as any action that threatened an endangered species; areas vital to a species' survival could be federally protected as "critical habitats" Though these definitions legislated strong environ-mentalist goals, political compromises made in the enforcement of the act were to determine just what economic interests would be set aside for the sake of ecological stabilization.

24. According to the passage, which of the following does the Endangered Species Act define as a "ritical habitat"

(A) A natural ecosystem that is threatened by imminent development

(B) An industrial or urban area in which wildlife species have almost ceased to live among humans

(C) A natural area that is crucial to the survival of a species and thus eligible for federal protection

(D) A wilderness area in which the "aking" of wildlife species is permitted rarely and only under strict federal regulation

(E) A natural environment that is protected under law because its wildlife has a high economic value

25. According to the passage, which of the following is an explanation for the degree of support that the Endangered Species Act received in Congress?

(A) Concern for the environment had gained increasing national popularity.

(B) Ecological research had created new economic opportunities dependent on the survival of certain species.

(C) Congress had long wanted to change the existing wildlife policy.

(D) The growth of industry had endangered increasing numbers of wildlife species.

(E) Legislators did not anticipate that the act could be effectively enforced.

笔 记 区

26. It can be inferred from the passage that if business interests had won the debate on provisions of the 1973 Endangered Species Act, which of the following would have resulted?

(A) Environmentalist concepts would not have become widely popular.

(B) The definitions of key terms of the act would have been more restricted.

(C) Enforcement of the act would have been more difficult.

(D) The act would have had stronger support from Congressional leaders.

(E) The public would have boycotted the industries that had the greatest impact in defining the act.

27. The author refers to the terms "wildlife"(line 7), "Taking"(line 8), and "critical habitats"(line 10) most likely in order to

(A) Illustrate the misuse of scientific language and concepts in political processes

(B) Emphasize the importance of selecting precise language in transforming scientific concepts into law

(C) Represent terminology whose definition was crucial in writing environmentalist goals into law

(D) Demonstrate the triviality of the issues debated by industries before Congress passed the Endangered Species Act

(E) Show that broad definitions of key terms in many types of laws resulted in ambiguity and thus left room for disagreement about how the law should be enforced

28. SWERVE:

(A) maintain direction

(B) resume operation

(C) slow down

(D) divert

(E) orient

29. HUSBAND:

(A) rearrange

(B) alarm

(C) assist

(D) prize

(E) squander

30. DEACTIVATE:

(A) palpate

(B) alleviate

(C) inhale

(D) articulate

笔 记 区

(E) potentiate

31. INTRANSIGENT:
(A) accustomed to command
(B) qualified to arbitrate
(C) open to compromise
(D) resigned to conflict
(E) opposed to violence

32. OCCLUDED:
(A) unvaried
(B) entire
(C) functional
(D) inverted
(E) unobstructed

33. ASSUAGE:
(A) intensify
(B) accuse
(C) correct
(D) create
(E) assert

34. QUIXOTIC:
(A) displaying consistently practical behavior
(B) considering several points of view
(C) expressing dissatisfaction
(D) suggesting uneasiness
(E) acting decisively

35. PELLUCID:
(A) stagnant
(B) murky
(C) glutinous
(D) noxious
(E) rancid

36. LACONISM:
(A) temerity
(B) vacuity
(C) dishonesty

笔 记 区

(D) immaturity
(E) verbosity

37. REFRACTORY:
(A) active
(B) productive
(C) energetic
(D) responsive
(E) powerful

38. DEFINITIVE:
(A) prosaic
(B) convoluted
(C) unusual
(D) provisional
(E) vast

SECTION 4

Time-30 minute 38 Questions

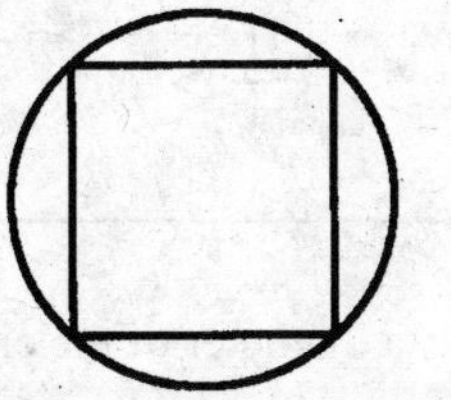

The square is inscribed in the circle.

1. The length of a diameter of the circle | The length of a diagonal of the square

---

$$\frac{3}{4}k=\frac{1}{8}$$

2. k | $\frac{1}{6}$

$$x-y=y-x$$

3. $x-y$ | 0

In a certain store, each record costs X dollars and each tape costs Y dollars. The total cost of 3 records and 2 tapes is \$39.

4. The cost of 1 record | The cost of 1 tape

The perimeter of rectangle $RSTU$ is 750, and RS =350.

5. ST | 50

---

6. $\frac{1}{2.}$ | 0.4

5

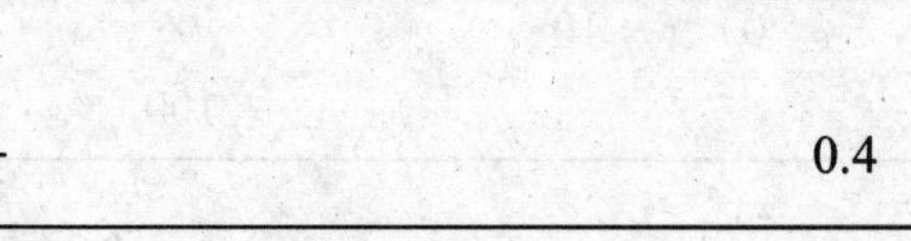

7. x 140

$$S = 1-\frac{1}{2}+\frac{1}{3}-\frac{1}{4}+\frac{1}{5}-\frac{1}{6}+\frac{1}{7}-\frac{1}{8}+\frac{1}{9}-\frac{1}{10}$$

8. S $\frac{1}{2}$

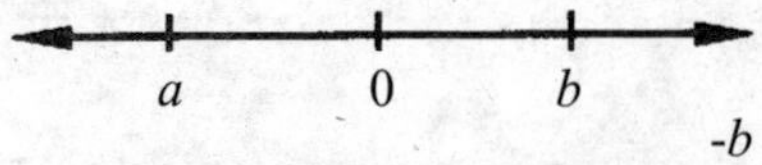

9. a $-b$

$$2-\frac{1}{x}>2$$

10. x 1

AB is a diameter of the circle.

11. The length of *AB* | The average (arithmetic mean) of the lengths of *AC* and *AD*

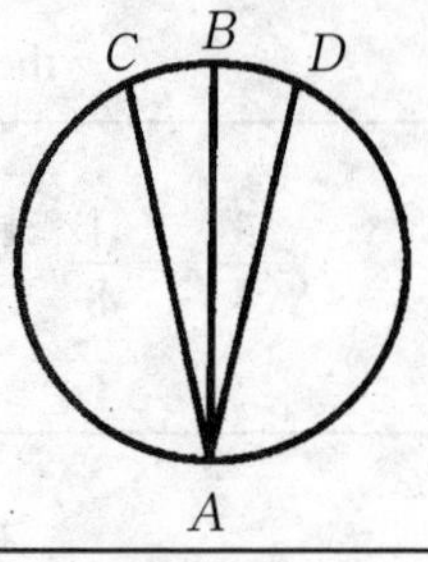

$0<x<y<1$

12. $1-y$ $y-x$

13. $\frac{1}{\sqrt{5}}[(\frac{1+\sqrt{5}}{2})-(\frac{1-\sqrt{5}}{2})]$ 1

$$y=x+\frac{1}{x}$$

$$0<x<10$$

14. The value of y 100

At a sale, the cost of each tie was reduced by 20 percent and the cost of each belt was reduced by 30 percent.

15. The percent reduction on the total cost of 1 tie and 2 belts 25%

16. $\frac{18}{60}(0.1254) =$

(A) 0.00522

(B) 0.03135

(C) 0.03762

(D) 0.0418

(E) 0.0627

17. What percent of the integers between 100 and 999, inclusive, have all three digits the same?

(A) 1%

(B) 2%

(C) 3%

(D) 4%

(E) 5%

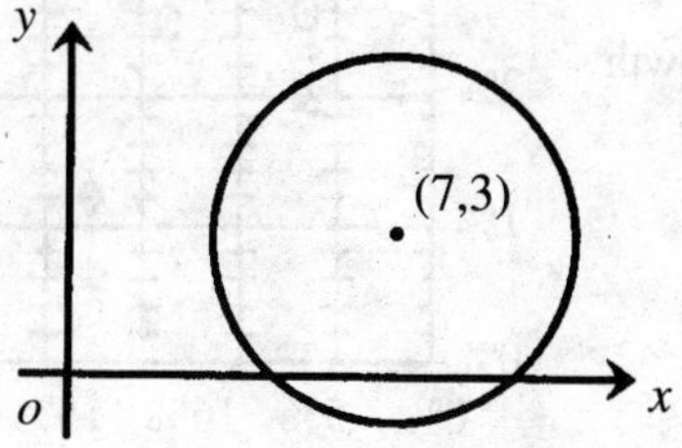

18. If (7, 3) is the center of the circle above, then the radius of the circle could be equal to which of the following?

(A) 2

(B) 3

(C) 5

(D) 7

(E) 9

19. If revenues \$196,000 from division A of Company *X* represent 28 percent of the total revenues of Company *X* for the year, What were the total revenues of Company *X* for the year?

(A) \$141,100

(B) \$272,000

(C) \$413,300

(D) \$596,100

(E) \$700,000

20. If $xy \neq 0$, which of the following is equivalent to $(\frac{x}{y})^3(\frac{2y}{x})^4$?

(A) $2xy$

(B) $8xy^2$

(C) $16x^2y^3$

(D) $\frac{2y}{x}$

(E) $\frac{16y}{x}$

笔 记 区

Questions 21-25 refer to the following graph.

AVERAGE ANNUAL NATIONAL SAVINGS RATE AND REAL GROSS NATIONAL PRODUCT (GNP) GROWTHRATE FOR SELECTED COUNTRIES

197161985

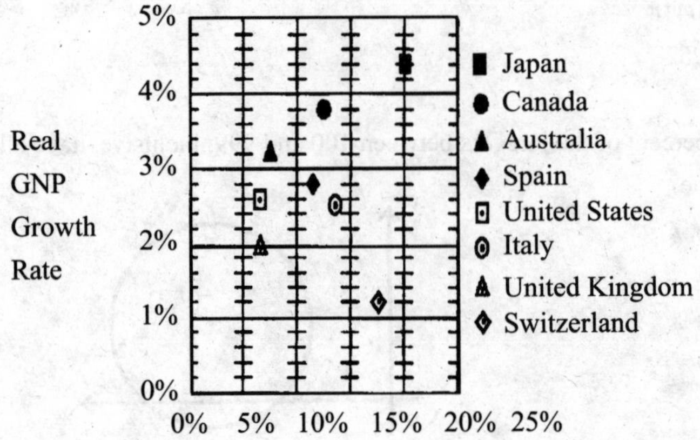

Savings Rate

(total savings as a percent of total personal income)

Note: Drawn to scale.

21. What was the savings rate for the country that had the greatest real GNP growth rate?

(A) 25%

(B) 20%

(C) 18%

(D) 12.5%

(E) 4.5%

22. For which country was the ratio of its savings rate to its real GNP growth rate greatest?

(A) Japan

(B) Canada

(C) Australia

(D) Italy

(E) Switzerland

23. The savings rate for Canada was approximately how many times that of the United States?

(A) $1\frac{1}{2}$

(B) 2

(C) $2\frac{1}{2}$

笔 记 区

(D) 3

(E) $3\frac{1}{2}$

24. For how many of the countries shown was the savings rate more than 5 times the real GNP growth rate?
(A) Five
(B) Four
(C) Three
(D) Two
(E) One

25. Which of the following statement can be inferred from the graph?
Ⅰ. On the average, people in the United States saved about the same amount as people in the United Kingdom.
II. The median of the savings rates for the eight countries was greater than 11 percent.
Ⅲ. Only two of the countries had a higher savings rate than Italy.
(A) Ⅰ only
(B) II only
(C) Ⅲ only
(D) Ⅰ and II
(E) IIand Ⅲ

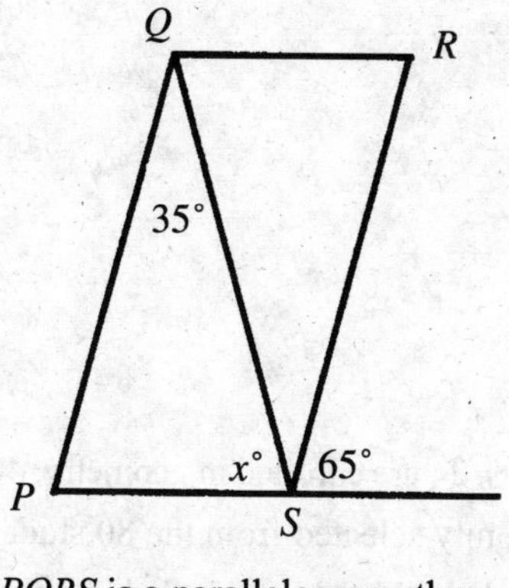

26. In the figure above, if *PQRS* is a parallelogram, then x =
(A) 35
(B) 65
(C) 75
(D) 80
(E) 100

27. A certain doctor suggests that an individual's daily water intake be $\frac{1}{2}$ ounce per pound of body weight plus 8 ounces for every 25 pounds by which the individual exceeds his or her ideal weight. If this doctor suggests a daily water intake of 136 ounces for a particular 240-pound individual, how many pounds above his or her ideal weight is that individual?

(A) $12\frac{1}{2}$
(B) 16
(C) 30
(D) 50
(E) 120

28. A political poll showed that 80 percent of those polled said they would vote for proposition P. Of those who said they would vote for proposition P 70 percent actually voted for P, and of those who did not say they would vote for P, 20 percent actually voted for P. What percent of those polled voted for P ?
(A) 56%
(B) 60%
(C) 64%
(D) 76%
(E) 90%

29. If $x \neq 1$ and $x \neq 0$, then $\frac{1-\frac{1}{x}}{x-1}$ is equivalent to
(A) $\frac{1}{x}$
(B) x
(C) $\frac{x}{1-x}$
(D) $\frac{x-1}{x}$
(E) $\frac{(x-1)^2}{x}$

30. In a group of 80 students, 24 are enrolled in geometry, 40 in biology, and 20 in both. If a student were randomly selected from the 80 students, what is the probability that the student selected would <u>not</u> be enrolled in either course?
(A) 0.20
(B) 0.25
(C) 0.45
(D) 0.55
(E) 0.60

SECTION 5
Time-30 minute 38 Questions

1. That she seemed to prefer______to concentrated effort is undeniable; nevertheless, the impressive quality of her finished paintings suggests that her actual relationship to her art was anything but______.
(A) preparation...passionate
(B) artfulness...disengaged
(C) dabbling...superficial
(D) caprice...considered
(E) indecision...lighthearted

2. Because of the excellent preservation of the fossil, anatomical details of early horseshoe crabs were______for the first time, enabling experts to______the evolution of the horseshoe crab.
(A) scrutinized...ensure
(B) verified...advance
(C) identified...distort
(D) obscured...illustrate
(E) clarified...reassess

3. The philosopher claimed that a person who must consciously______his or her own indifference before helping another is behaving more nobly than one whose basic disposition allows such an act to be performed without______.
(A) feign...enthusiasm
(B) censure...comment
(C) embrace...duplicity
(D) suffer...effort
(E) overcome...deliberation

4. The senator's attempt to convince the public that he is not interested in running for a second term is______given the extremely______fund-raising activities of his campaign committee.

笔记区

(A) futile...clandestine

(B) sincere...visible

(C) specious...apathetic

(D) disingenuous...public

(E) straightforward...dubious

5. Although a change in management may appear to______a shift in a company' s fortunes, more often than not its impact is_______.

(A) hinder...measurable

(B) promote...demonstrable

(C) accelerate...profound

(D) betray...fundamental

(E) augur...inconsiderable

6. The skeleton of______bird that was recently discovered indicated that this ancient creature______today' s birds in that, unlike earlier birds and unlike reptilian ancestors, it had not a tooth in its head.

(A) a primeval...obscured

(B) a unique...preempted

(C) a primitive...anticipated

(D) a contemporary...foreshadowed

(E) an advanced...differed from

7. While many people utilize homeopathic remedies to treat health problems, other people do not______such alternative treatments,______conventional medical treatments instead.

(A) distrust...employing

(B) embrace...eschewing

(C) reject...envisioning

(D) countenance...relying on

(E) recommend...turning from

8. PROGRAM: CONCERT::

(A) bibliography : book

(B) menu : entree

(C) questionnaire : poll

(D) platform : campaign

(E) agenda : meeting

9. EMBRACE: AFFECTION::

(A) prediction : memory

(B) innuendo : secrecy

笔 记 区

(C) shrug : indifference
(D) conversation : familiarity
(E) vote : unanimity

10. ENTHUSIASM : MANIA::
(A) idea : inspiration
(B) nightmare : hallucination
(C) failure : disgust
(D) suspicion : paranoia
(E) energy : fitness

11. ANONYMOUS : IDENTIFY::
(A) nonchalant : excite
(B) repressed : constrain
(C) misled : trust
(D) annoying : assist
(E) unremarkable : please

12. CARTOGRAPHER : MAP::
(A) astronomer : stars
(B) carpenter: wood
(C) lumberjack : saw
(D) tailor : clothing
(E) weaver : loom

13. EXEMPLARY: IMITATION::
(A) venerable : denigration
(B) novel : duplication
(C) redoubtable : regard
(D) challenging : determination
(E) creditable: verification

14. INSENSITIVE:BOOR::
(A) spontaneous : extrovert
(B) mischievous : imp
(C) conformist : ally
(D) officious : zealot
(E) extravagant : miser

15. LABYRINTHINE : SIMPLICITY::
(A) epic : scope

笔 记 区

(B) digressive : motive

(C) heretical : sincerity

(D) austere : design

(E) jejune : interest

16. EUPHEMISM:OFFENSIVE::

(A) rhetoric : persuasive

(B) aphorism : diffuse

(C) metaphor : descriptive

(D) repetition : fatiguing

(E) conciliation : appeasing

From the 1900ís through the 1950ís waitresses in the United States developed a form of unionism based on the unionsí defining the skills that their occupation included and enforcing standards for the performance of those skills. This ìoccupational unionismî differed substantially from the ìworksite unionismî prevalent among factory workers. Rather than unionizing the workforces of particular employers, waitress locals sought to control their occupation throughout a city. Occupational unionism operated through union hiring halls, which provided free placement services to employers who agreed to hire their personnel only through the union. Hiring halls offered union waitresses collective employment security, not individual job securityó a basic protection offered by worksite unions. That is, when a waitress lost her job, the local did not intervene with her employer but placed her elsewhere; and when jobs were scarce, the work hours available were distributed fairly among all members rather than being assigned according to seniority.

17. The primary purpose of the passage is to

(A) analyze a current trend in relation to the past

(B) discuss a particular solution to a long-standing problem

(C) analyze changes in the way that certain standards have been enforced

(D) apply a generalization to an unusual situation

(E) describe an approach by contrasting it with another approach

18. Which of the following statements best summarizes a distinction mentioned in the passage between waitress unions and factory workers' unions?

(A) Waitress unions were more successful than factory workers' unions in that they were able to unionize whole cities.

(B) Waitress unions had an impact on only certain local areas, whereas the impact of factory workers' unions was national.

(C) Waitress union members held primarily part-time positions, whereas factory workers' unions placed their members in full-time jobs.

(D) Waitress unions emphasized the occupation of workers, whereas factory workers' unions emphasized the worksite at which workers were employed.

(E) Waitress unions defined the skills of their trade, whereas the skills of factory trades were determined by employers' groups.

19. According to the passage, which of the following was characteristic of the form of union that United States waitresses developed in the first half of the twentieth century?

(A) The union represented a wide variety of restaurant and hotel service occupations.

(B) The union defined the skills required of waitresses and disciplined its members to meet certain standards.

(C) The union billed employers for its members' work and distributed the earnings among all members.

(D) The union negotiated the enforcement of occupational standards with each employer whose workforce joined the union.

(E) The union ensured that a worker could not be laid off arbitrarily by an employer.

20. The author of the passage mentions "particular employers"(line 5) primarily in order to

(A) suggest that occupational unions found some employers difficult to satisfy

(B) indicate that the occupational unions served some employers but not others

(C) emphasize the unique focus of occupational unionism

(D) accentuate the hostility of some employers toward occupational unionism

(E) point out a weakness of worksite unionism

In prehistoric times brachiopods were one of the most abundant and diverse forms of life on Earth: more han 30,000 species of this clamlike creature have been cataloged from fossil records. Today brachiopods are not as numerous, and existing species are not well studied, partly because neither the animalís fleshy inner tissue nor its shell has any commercial value. Moreover, in contrast to the greater diversity of the extinct species, the approximately 300 known surviving species are relatively, uniform in appearance. Many zoologists have interpreted this as a sign that the animal has been unable to compete successfully with other marine organisms in the evolutionary struggle.

Several things, however, suggest that the conven tional view needs revising. For example, the genus Lingula has an unbroken fossil record extending over more than half a billion years to the present. Thus, if longevity is any measure, brachiopods are the most successful organisms extant. Further, recent studies suggest that diversity among species is a less important measure of evolutionary success than is the ability to withstand environmental change, such as when a layer of clay replaces sand on the ocean bottom. The relatively greater uniformity among the existing brachiopod species

笔 记 区

may offer greater protection from environmental change and hence may reflect highly successful adaptive behavior.

The adaptive advantages of uniformity for brachiopods can be seen by considering specialization, a process that occurs as a result of prolonged colonization of a uniform substrate. Those that can survive on many surfaces are called generalists, while those that can survive on a limited range of substrates are called specialists. One specialist species, for example, has valves weighted at the base, a characteristic that assures that the organism is properly positioned for feeding in mud and similar substrates; other species secrete glue allowing them to survive on the face of underwater cliffs. The fossil record demonstrates that most brachiopod lineages have followed a trend toward increased specialization. However, during periods of environmental instability, when a particular substrate to which a specialist species has adapted is no longer available, the species quickly dies out. Generalists, on the other hand, are not dependent on a particular substrate, and are thus less vulnerable to environmental change. One study of the fossil record revealed a mass extinction of brachiopods following a change in sedimentation from chalk to clay. Of the 35 brachiopod species found in the chalk, only 6 survived in the clay, all of them generalists.

As long as enough generalist species are maintained, and studies of arctic and subarctic seas suggest that generalists are often dominant members of the marine communities there, it seems unlikely that the phylum is close to extinction.

21. In the passage, the author is primarily concerned with
   (A) rejecting an earlier explanation for the longevity of certain brachiopod species
   (B) reevaluating the implications of uniformity among existing brachiopod species
   (C) describing the varieties of environmental change to which brachiopods are vulnerable
   (D) reconciling opposing explanations for brachiopods' lack of evolutionary success
   (E) elaborating the mechanisms responsible for the tendency among brachiopod species toward specialization

22. It can be inferred from the passage that many zoologists assume that a large diversity among species of a given class of organisms typically leads to which of the following?
   (A) Difficulty in classification
   (B) A discontinuous fossil record
   (C) A greater chance of survival over time
   (D) Numerical abundance
   (E) A longer life span

23. The second paragraph makes use of which of the following?
   (A) Specific examples

笔 记 区

(B) Analogy
(C) Metaphor
(D) Quotation
(E) Exaggeration

24. The author suggests that the scientists holding the conventional view mentioned in lines 9-10 make which of the following errors?
(A) They mistakenly emphasize survival rather than diversity.
(B) They misunderstand the causes of specialization.
(C) They misuse zoological terminology.
(D) They catalog fossilized remains improperly.
(E) They overlook an alternative criterion of evolutionary success.

25. It can be inferred from the passage that the decision to study an organism may sometimes be influenced by
(A) its practical or commercial benefits to society
(B) the nature and prevalence of its fossilized remains
(C) the relative convenience of its geographical distribution
(D) its similarity to one or more better-known species
(E) the degree of its physiological complexity

26. Which of the following, if true, would most strengthen the author' s claim (lines 34-35) that it seems unlikely that the phylum is close to extinction"?
(A) Generalist species now living in arctic water give few if any indications of a tendency towards significant future specialization.
(B) Zoologists have recently discovered that a common marine organism is a natural predator of brachiopods.
(C) It was recently discovered that certain brachiopod species are almost always concentrated near areas rich in offshore oil deposits.
(D) The ratio of specialist to generalist species is slowly but steadily increasing.
(E) It is easier for a brachiopod to survive a change in sedimentation than a change in water temperature.

27. Information in the passage supports which of the following statements about brachiopods?
Ⅰ. Few brachiopods living in prehistoric times were specialists.
II. A tendency toward specialization, though typical, is not inevitable.
Ⅲ. Specialist species dominate in all but arctic and subarctic waters.
(A) I only
(B) II only
(C) II and III only

笔记区

(D) I and III only
(E) I, II and III

28. MISREAD:
(A) refocus
(B) approve
(C) predict
(D) explain succinctly
(E) interpret correctly

29. DISSIPATE:
(A) gather
(B) seethe
(C) relax
(D) exert
(E) incite

30. ENUNCIATE:
(A) mumble
(B) disclaim
(C) dissuade
(D) bluster
(E) commend

31. TAUTEN:
(A) rarefy
(B) coarsen
(C) force
(D) loosen
(E) constrain

32. ZEALOTRY:
(A) pessimism
(B) generosity
(C) gullibility
(D) lack of fervor
(E) excess of confidence

33. REDOLENT
(A) cheerful
(B) resolute

笔 记 区

(C) unscented
(D) uncovered
(E) untainted

34. GLUTINOUS:
(A) nonviscous
(B) nonporous
(C) antitoxic
(D) catalytic
(E) alkaline

35. PANEGYRIC:
(A) covenant
(B) recantation
(C) enigma
(D) termination
(E) anathema

36. AWASH:
(A) fouled
(B) quenched
(C) rigid
(D) dry
(E) sturdy

37. UNTOWARD:
(A) direct
(B) fortunate
(C) tangential
(D) decisive
(E) effective

38. SUPERCILIOUS.
(A) castigating
(B) obsequious
(C) reclusive
(D) rambunctious
(E) abrasive

笔 记 区

SECTION 6

Time-30 minute 30 Questions

$2x-1>0$

1. x	$\frac{1}{4}$

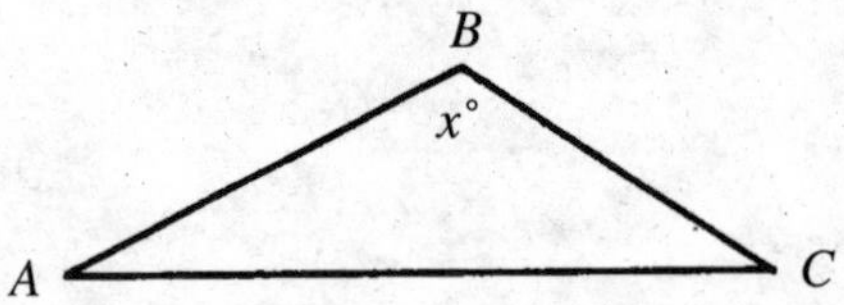

$x > 90$

2. The perimeter of ABC	3 times the length of AC
3. The total area of 18 nonoverlapping circular regions, each having a diameter of 2 inches	36 square inches

$0<p<1$

4. The greatest value of $p\ (1-p)$	$\frac{1}{2}$

S is the sum of the first n negative integer powers of 2;
i.e., $S = 2^{-1} + 2^{-2} + \ldots + 2^{-n}$

5. S	1

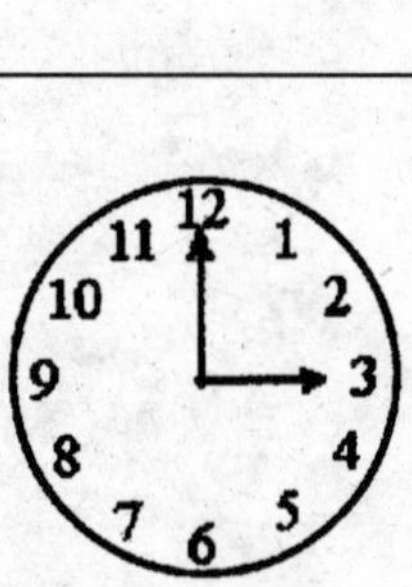

The minute hand of a tower clock is 3 feet long and the hour hand is 2 feet long. The two hands are in the three o' lock position, as shown.

6. The distance between the tips of the two hands of the clock — 4 feet

---

s and t are integers, $s>t$, and $t \neq 0$.

7. $\frac{s}{t}$ — s

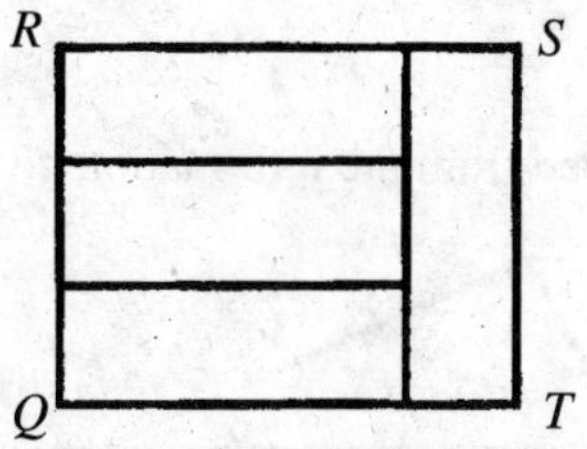

Rectangular region *QRST* is divided into four smaller rectangular regions, each with length 1 and width *w*.

8. $\frac{QR}{RS}$ — $\frac{3}{4}$

---

9. $(5)^0(-3)^0$ — 0

---

10. $\frac{6}{\sqrt{3}}$ — $2\sqrt{3}$

$xy+y^2=3$

11. x — y

---

12. $\frac{0.205}{0.305}$ — $\frac{2}{3}$

$x-1=y$

13. $1-x$ — y

The 20 people at a party are divided into *n* mutually exclusive groups in such a way that the number of people in any group does not exceed the number in any other group by more than 1.

14. The value of *n* if at least one of the groups consists of 3 people — 6

For the line with equation $y=ax+b$, $ab \neq 0$, the *x*-intercept is twice the *y*-intercept.

15. The slope of the line $\frac{1}{2}$

---

16. If $x+y=x$, what is the value of y?

(A) −2

(B) −1

(C) 0

(D) 2

(E) It cannot be determined from the information given.

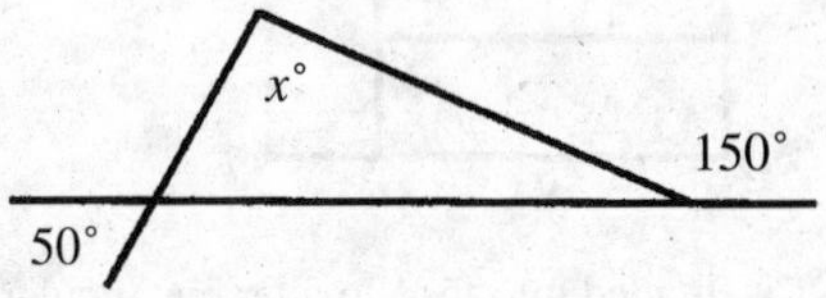

17. In the figure above, x =

(A) 30

(B) 80

(C) 100

(D) 130

(E) 160

18. The average (arithmetic mean) number of trees per acre in a 40-acre plot is 140. If a 10-acre section of the plot contains 90 trees per acre, how many trees are there in the remaining 30 acres?

(A) 5,700

(B) 4,700

(C) 4,200

(D) 3,600

(E) 2,700

19. Which of the following sums is greater than 1?

(A) $\frac{1}{2}+\frac{1}{3}$

(B) $\frac{7}{8}+\frac{3}{30}$

(C) $\frac{15}{16}+\frac{2}{40}$

(D) $\frac{12}{25}+\frac{12}{30}$

(E) $\frac{35}{102}+\frac{2}{3}$

20. If the vertices of a triangle have rectangular coordinates (0,0), (8,0), and (8,6), respectively, then the perimeter of the triangle is

(A) 10

(B) 14

(C) 24

(D) 36

(E) 48

<u>Questions 21-25</u> refer to the following graphs.

AVERAGE VEHICLE OCCUPANCY RATE FOR COMMUTERS TO CTTY P AND ITS SIX SUBURBAN COUNTIES

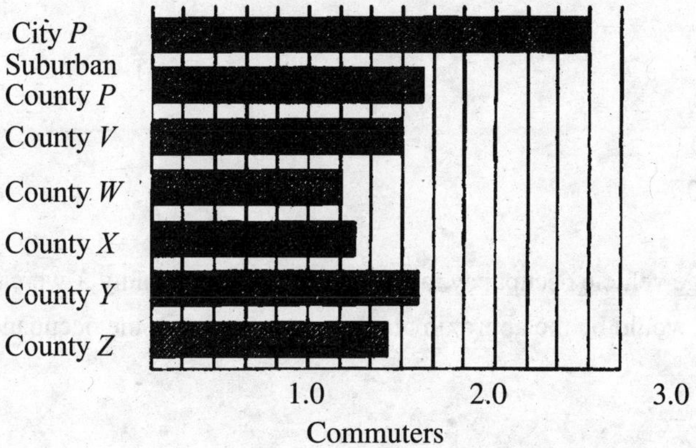

Note: Drawn to scale.

MEANS OF TRAVEL FOR COMMUTERS TO CITY *P*

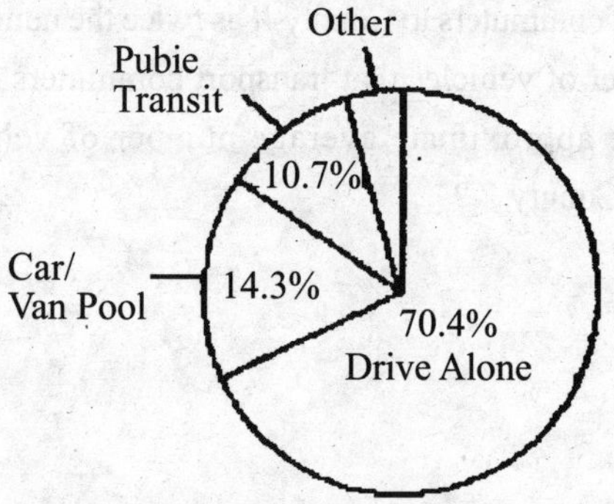

21. For how many of the areas listed was the average vehicle occupancy rate for commuters less than 1.8?

(A) Seven

(B) Six

(C) Five

(D) Four

(E) Three

22. The average vehicle occupancy rate for commuters to County *Y* is most nearly

(A) 1.3

(B) 1.4

(C) 1.5

(D) 1.6

(E) 1.7

23. Of the 2 million people who commute to City *P*, approximately how many travel by public transit?

(A) 21,400

(B) 140,000

(C) 214,000

(D) 286,000

(E) 2,140,000

24. If the average vehicle occupancy rate for commuters to County *X* were to increase to 2.8, what would be the approximate percent increase in the occupancy rate?

(A) 46%

(B) 54%

(C) 87%

(D) 115%

(E) 215%

25. If the total number of commuters to County *W* is twice the number to County *Z*, and if the average number of vehicles that transport commuters daily to County *W* is 30,000, what is the approximate average number of vehicles that transport commuters daily to County *Z*?

(A) 12,000

(B) 15,000

(C) 18,000

(D) 27,000

(E) 36,000

26. If the average (arithmetic mean) of k and $7k$ is 60, then $k =$

(A) 6

(B) 7.5

(C) 8

(D) 9.5
(E) 15

27. In a crate of fruit that contained strawberries, blueberries, and raspberries, the ratio of the number of pints of strawberries to the number of pints of blueberries to the number of pints of raspberries was 6 to 4 to 5, respectively. If the crate contained a total of 45 pints of these fruits, how many more pints of strawberries than blueberries were there in the crate?

(A) 2
(B) 3
(C) 4
(D) 5
(E) 6

28. For a project, a square piece of cloth is folded in half and sewed together to form a rectangle that has a perimeter of 36 centimeters, What was the area in square centimeters of the piece of cloth before it was folded?

(A) 16
(B) 36
(C) 81
(D) 108
(E) 144

29. How many positive 4-digit integers begin (on the left) with an odd digit and end with an even digit?

(A) 250
(B) 500
(C) 2,000
(D) 2,500
(E) 5,000

30. For a certain farm, soybean production increased by 25 percent from year X to year Y, and the selling price of soybeans decreased by 25 percent from year X to year Y. If the entire soybean production was sold each year, approximately what was the percent change in the revenues from the sale of the soybeans from year X to year Y?

(A) 56% decrease
(B) 6% decrease
(C) No change
(D) 6% increase
(E) 56% increase

笔 记 区

五、最新GRE 笔试模考练习题五

SECTION 1

Time-45 minutes

ISSUE TASK

Present your perspective on the issue you choose from the two topics below, using relevant reasons and /or examples to support your views

Topic 1:

"Although, critics who write about the arts tend to deny the existence of any objective standards for evaluating works of art, they have a responsibility to establish standards by which works of art can be judged."

Topic 2:

"It is possible to pass laws that control or place limits on people's behavior, but legislation cannot reform human nature. Laws cannot change what is in people's hearts and minds"

SECTION 2

Time-30 minute

Argument task

Discuss how well reasoned you find this argument.

The following appeared in a memo at the XYZ company.

"Among all students who graduated from Hooper University over the past five years, more physical science majors than social science majors found permanent jobs within a year of graduation. In a survey of recent Hooper University graduates, most physical science majors said they believed that the prestige of Hooper University's physical science programs helped them significantly in finding a job. In contrast, social science majors who found permanent employment attributed their success to their own personal initiative. Therefore, to ensure that social science majors find permanent jobs, Hooper University should offer additional social science courses and hire several new faculty members who already have national reputations in the social sciences."

笔 记 区

SECTION 3

Time-30 minute 30 Questions

$$5y = 15$$
$$x = 2y$$

1.	x	5

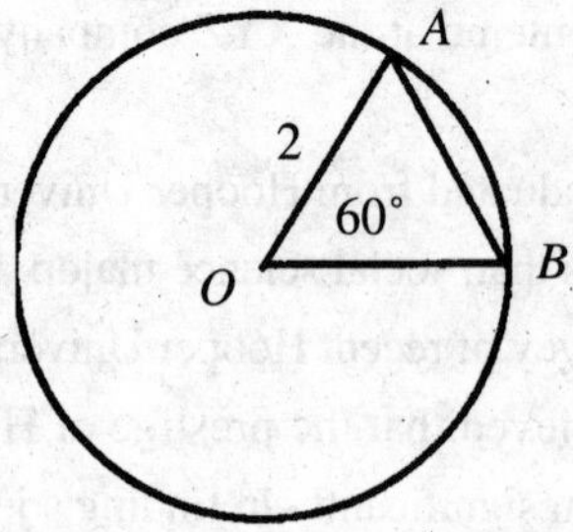

O is the center of the circle and the perimeter of $\triangle AOB$ is 6.

2.	The circumference of the circle	12

Ken's monthly take-home pay is w dollars. After he pays for food and rent, he has x dollars left

3.	x	$w-x$
4.	$\dfrac{\frac{13}{15}+\frac{7}{8}+\frac{3}{4}}{3}$	1

$$(x-2y)(x+2y)=4$$

5.	x^2-4y^2	8
6.	$\dfrac{0.3}{1.5}$	$\dfrac{2}{10}$

The operation ◆ is defined for all positive numbers r and t by $r ◆ t = \frac{(r-t)^2+rt}{t}$

7.	71◆37	37◆71

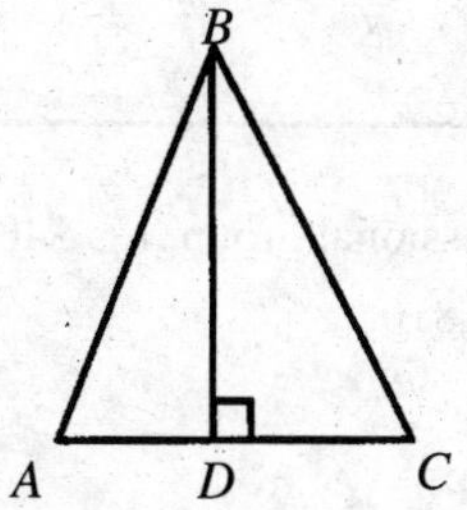

8.	$\frac{BD}{AB}$	$\frac{DC}{BC}$
9.	(250)(492)	$\frac{492,000}{4}$

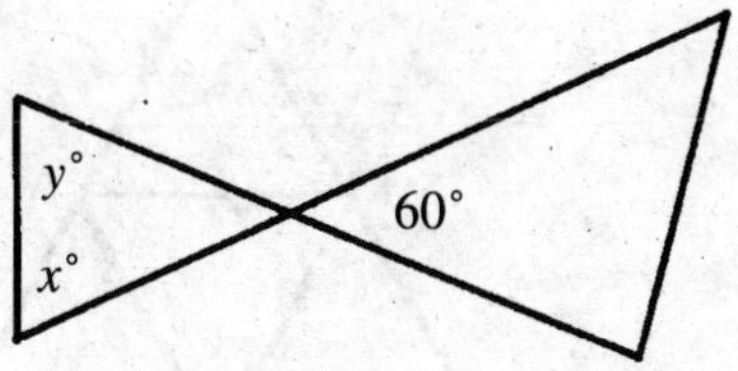

10.	x	y
11.	The number of prime numbers between 70 and 76	The number of prime numbers between 30 and 36

$6 < x < 7$

$y = 8$

12.	$\frac{x}{y}$	0.85

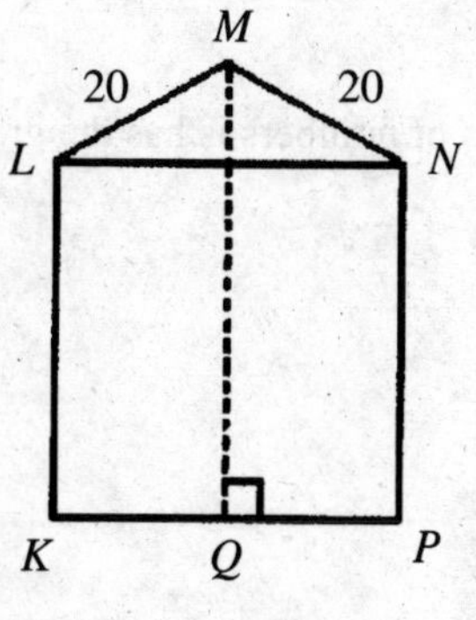

笔 记 区

KLNP is a square with perimeter 128.

13.	*MQ*	42
14.	$\frac{2+3x}{2}$	$1+3x$

The median salary for professional group *A* is \$40,610. The median salary for professional group *B* is \$40,810.

15. The median salary for groups *A* and *B* combined	\$40,710

16. The water level in a tank is lowered by 6 inches, then raised by $8\frac{1}{2}$ inches, and then lowered by 4 inches. If the water level was *x* inches before the changes in level, which of the following represents the water level, in inches, after the changes?

(A) $x-1\frac{1}{2}$

(B) $x+1\frac{1}{2}$

(C) $x-6\frac{1}{2}$

(D) $x+6\frac{1}{2}$

(E) $x-18\frac{1}{2}$

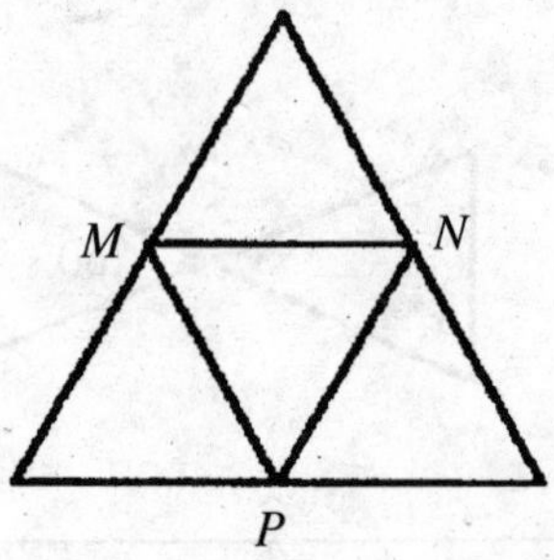

17. In the figure above, *M*, *N*, and *P* are midpoints of the sides of an equilateral triangle whose perimeter is 18. What is the perimeter of the shaded region?

(A) 2

(B) 3

(C) $4\frac{1}{2}$

(D) 6

(E) 9

18. Which of the following sets of numbers is has the greatest standard deviation?

(A) 2, 3, 4

(B) 2.5, 3, 3.5

(C) 1, 1.25, 1.5

(D) −2, 0, 2

(E) 20, 21, 21.5

笔 记 区

19. If x, y, and z represent consecutive integers, and $x<y<z$, which of the following equals y?

Ⅰ. $x+1$

II. $\frac{x+z}{2}$

III. $\frac{x+y+z}{3}$

(A) Ⅰ only

(B) Ⅰ and Ⅱ only

(C) Ⅰ and Ⅲ only

(D) Ⅱ and Ⅲ only

(E) Ⅰ, Ⅱand Ⅲ

20. When 9 students took a zoology quiz with a possible score of 0 to 10, inclusive, there average (arithmetic mean) score was 7.5. If a tenth student takes the same quiz, what will be the least possible average score on the quiz for all 10 students?

(A) 6.5

(B) 6.75

(C) 7.0

(D) 7.25

(E) 7.5

<u>Questions 21-25</u> refer to the following graph.

CORPORATE SUPPORT FOR THE ARTS BY SECTOR IN 1988 AND 1991

Total for 1988 $630 million

Total for 1991 $520 million

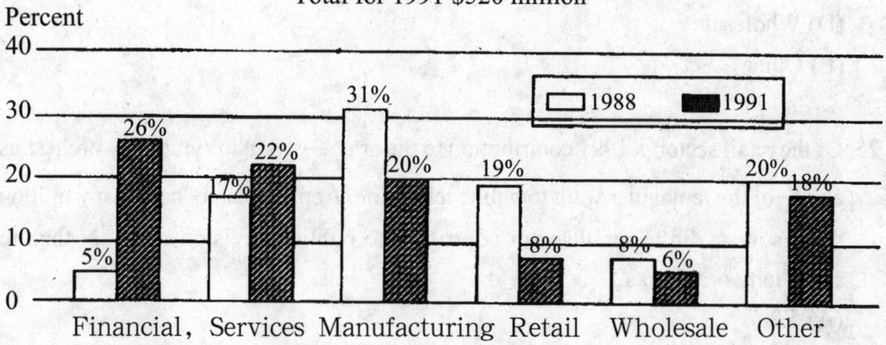

21. The two corporate sectors that increased their support for the arts from 1988 to 1991 made a total contribution in 1991 of approximately how many million dollars?

(A) 112

(B) 125

(C) 200

(D) 250

(E) 315

22. How many of the six corporate sectors listed each contributed more than $60 million to the arts in both 1988 and 1991?

(A) One

(B) Two

(C) three

(D) Four

(E) Five

23. Approximately how many million dollars more did the wholesale sector contribute to the arts in 1988 than in 1991?

(A) 10.4

(B) 12.6

(C) 14.0

(D) 16.5

(E) 19.2

24. From 1988 to 1991, which corporate sector decreased its support for the arts by the greatest dollar amount?

(A) Services

(B) Manufacturing

(C) Retail

(D) Wholesale

(E) Other

25. Of the retail sector's 1991 contribution to the arts, $\frac{1}{4}$ went to symphony orchestras and $\frac{1}{2}$ of the remainder went to public television. Approximately how many million dollars more did to retail sector contribute to public television that year than to symphony orchestras?

(A) 5.2

(B) 6.3

(C) 10.4

(D) 13.0

(E) 19.5

26. If $x = a^5$ and $y = a^6$, $a \neq 0$, which of the following is equivalent to a^{13}?

笔 记 区

(A) xy
(B) x^2y
(C) $\frac{x^2}{y}$
(D) $\frac{x^4}{y}$
(E) $\frac{y^3}{x}$

27. The probabilities that each of two independent experiments will have a successful outcome are $\frac{8}{15}$ and $\frac{2}{3}$, respectively. What is the probability that both experiments will have successful outcomes?

(A) $\frac{4}{5}$
(B) $\frac{6}{5}$
(C) $\frac{2}{15}$
(D) $\frac{16}{45}$
(E) $\frac{64}{225}$

28. If x is 1, 2, or 3 and y is either 2 or 4, then the product xy can have how many different possible values?

(A) Three
(B) Four
(C) Five
(E) Six
(E) Seven

29. If the radius of a circular region were decreased by 20 percent, the area of the circular region would decrease by what percent?

(A) 16%
(B) 20%
(C) 36%
(D) 40%
(E) 44%

30. Workers at Companies X and Y are paid the same base hourly rate. Workers at company X are paid 1.5 times the base hourly rate for each hour worked per week in excess of the first 37, while workers at Company Y are paid 1.5 times the base hourly rate for each hour worked per week in excess of the first 40. In a given week, how many hours

笔 记 区

must a Company *X* worker work in order to receive the same pay as a Company *Y* worker who works 46 hours?

(A) 46

(B) 45

(C) 44

(D) 43

(E) 42

SECTION 4

Time-30 minute 38 Questions

1. As businesses become aware that their advertising must _____ the everyday concerns of consumers, their commercials will be characterized by a greater degree of _____.
   (A) allay...pessimism
   (B) address...realism
   (C) evade...verisimilitude
   (D) engage...fancy
   (E) change...sincerity

2. Because the lawyer's methods were found to be _____, the disciplinary committee _____his privileges.
   (A) unimpeachable...suspended
   (B) ingenious...withdrew
   (C) questionable...expanded
   (D) unscrupulous...revoked
   (E) reprehensible...augmented

3. People of intelligence and achievement can nonetheless be so _____ and lacking in _____that they gamble their reputations by breaking the law to further their own ends.
   (A) devious...propensity
   (B) culpable...prosperity
   (C) obsequious...deference
   (D) truculent...independence
   (E) greedy...integrity

4. A number of scientists have published articles _____ global warming, stating _____ that there is no solid scientific evidence to support the theory that the Earth is warming because of increases in greenhouse gases.
   (A) debunking...categorically
   (B) rejecting...paradoxically
   (C) deploring...optimistically

(D) dismissing...hesitantly

(E) proving...candidly

5. The senator's attempt to convince the public that she is not interested in running for a second term is as ____ as her opponent's attempt to disguise his intention to run against her.

(A) biased

(B) unsuccessful

(C) inadvertent

(D) indecisive

(E) remote

6. MacCrory's conversation was ____: she could never tell a story, chiefly because she always forgot it, and she was never guilty of a witticism, unless by accident.

(A) scintillating

(B) unambiguous

(C) perspicuous

(D) stultifying

(E) facetious

7. Despite its many ____, the whole-language philosophy of teaching reading continues to gain ____ among educators.

(A) detractors...notoriety

(B) adherents...prevalence

(C) critics...currency

(D) enthusiasts...popularity

(E) practitioners...credibility

8. CENSUS: POPULATION::

(A) interrogation: guilt

(B) survey: price

(C) interview: personality

(D) questionnaire: explanation

(E) inventory: stock

9. AUTHENTICITY: FRAUDULENT::

(A) morality: utopian

(B) intensity: vigorous

(C) sincerity: hypocritical

(D) particularity: unique

(E) plausibility: narrated

笔 记 区

10. VARNISH: GLOSSY::
(A) sharpen: blunt
(B) measure: deep
(C) sand: smooth
(D) approximate: precise
(E) anchor: unstable

11. AMENITY: COMFORTABLE
(A) tact: circumspect
(B) nuisance: aggravated
(C) honorarium:grateful
(D) favorite: envious
(E) lounge: patient

12. PAIN: ANALGESIC::
(A) energy: revitalization
(B) interest: stimulation
(C) symptom: palliative
(D) despair: anxiety
(E) reward: incentive

13. VOICE:SHOUT::
(A) ear: overhear
(B) eye: see
(C) hand: clutch
(D) nerve: feel
(E) nose: inhale

14. PONTIFICATE: SPEAK::
(A) strut: walk
(B) stare: look
(C) patronize: frequent
(D) eulogize: mourn
(E) reciprocate: give

15. BIBLIOPHILE: BOOKS::
(A) environmentalist: pollution
(B) zoologist: animals
(C) gourmet: food
(D) calligrapher: handwriting
(E) aviator: aircraft

笔 记 区

16. INDIGENT: WEALTH::
(A) presumptuous: independence
(B) imperturbable: determination
(C) inevitable: inescapability
(D) indigestible: sustenance
(E) redundant: indispensability

This passage is based on an article published in 1990.

Eight times within the past million years, something in the Earth's climatic equation has changed, allowing snow in the mountains and the northern latitudes to accumulate from one season to the next instead of melting away. Each time, the enormous ice sheets resulting from this continual buildup lasted tens of thousands of years until the end of each particular glacial cycle brought a warmer climate. Scientists speculated that these glacial cycles were ultimately driven by astronomical factors: slow, cyclic changes in the eccentricity of the Earth's orbit and in the tilt and orientation of its spin axis. But up until around 30 years ago, the lack of an independent record of ice- age timing made the hypothesis untestable.

Then in the early 1950's Emiliani produced the first complete record of the waxings and wanings of past glaciations. It came from a seemingly odd place. the seafloor. Single-cell marine organisms called "foraminifera" house themselves in shells made from calcium carbonate. When the foraminifera die, sink to the bottom, and become part of seafloor sediments, the carbonate of their shells preserves certain characteristics of the seawater they inhabited. In particular, the ratio of a heavy isotope of oxygen (oxygen-18) to ordinary oxygen (oxygen-16) in the carbonate preserves the ratio of the two oxygens in water molecules.

It is now understood that the ratio of oxygen isotopes in seawater closely reflects the proportion of the world's water locked up in glaciers and ice sheets. A kind of meteorological distillation accounts for the link. Water molecules containing the heavier isotope tend to condense and fall as precipitation slightly sooner than molecules containing the lighter isotope. Hence, as water vapor evaporated from warm oceans moves away from its source, its oxygen-18 returns more quickly to the oceans than does its oxygen-16. What falls as snow on distant ice sheets and mountain glaciers is relatively depleted of oxygen-18. As the oxygen-18-poor ice builds up, the oceans become relatively enriched in the isotope. The larger the ice sheets grow, the higher the proportion of oxygen-18 becomes in seawater—and hence in the sediments.

Analyzing cores drilled from seafloor sediments, Emiliani found that the isotopic ratio rose and fell in rough accord with the Earth's astronomical cycles. Since that pioneering observation, oxygen-isotope measurements have been made on hundreds of cores. A chronology for the combined record enables scientists to show that the record contains the very same periodicities as the orbital processes. Over the past 800, 000 years, the global ice volume has peaked every 100,000 years, matching the period of the orbital eccentricity variation. In addition, "wrinkles" superposed on each cycle-

笔 记 区

small decreases or surges in ice volume-have come at intervals of roughly 23,000 and 41, 000 years, in keeping with the precession and tilt frequencies of the Earthís spin axis.

17. Which of the following best expresses the main idea of the passage?
   (A) Marine sediments have allowed scientists to amass evidence tending to confirm that astronomical cycles drive the Earthís glacial cycles.
   (B) The ratio between two different isotopes of oxygen in seawater correlates closely with the size of the Earthís ice sheets.
   (C) Surprisingly, single-cell marine organisms provide a record of the Earthís ice ages.
   (D) The Earthís astronomical cycles have recently been revealed to have an unexpectedly large impact on the Earthís climate.
   (E) The Earth has experienced eight periods of intense glaciation in the past million years, primarily as a result of substantial changes in its orbit.

18. The passage asserts that one reason that oceans become enriched in oxygen-18 as ice sheets grow is because
   (A) water molecules containing oxygen-18 condense and fall as precipitation slightly sooner than those containing oxygen-16
   (B) the ratio of oxygen-18 to oxygen-16 in water vapor evaporated from oceans is different from that of these isotopes in seawater
   (C) growing ice sheets tend to lose their oxygen-18 as the temperature of the oceans near them gradually decreases
   (D) less water vapor evaporates from oceans during glacial periods and therefore less oxygen-18 is removed from the seawater
   (E) the freezing point of seawater rich in oxygen-18 is slightly lower than that of seawater poor in oxygen-18

19. According to the passage,. the large ice sheets typical of glacial cycles are most directly caused by
   (A) changes in the average temperatures in the tropics and over open oceans
   (B) prolonged increases in the rate at which water evaporates from the oceans
   (C) extreme seasonal variations in temperature in northern latitudes and in mountainous areas
   (D) steadily increasing precipitation rates in northern latitudes and in mountainous areas
   (E) the continual failure of snow to melt completely during the warmer seasons in northern latitudes and in mountainous areas

20. It can be inferred from the passage that which of the following is true of the water locked in glaciers and ice sheets today?

(A) It is richer in oxygen-18 than frozen water was during past glacial periods.
(B) It is primarily located in the northern latitudes of the Earth.
(C) Its ratio of oxygen isotopes is the same as that prevalent in seawater during the last ice age.
(D) It is steadily decreasing in amount due to increased thawing during summer months.
(E) In comparison with seawater, it is relatively poor in oxygen-18.

21. The discussion of the oxygen-isotope ratios in paragraph three of the passage suggests that which of the following must be assumed if the conclusions described in lines 31-36 are to be validly drawn?
(A) The Earthís overall annual precipitation rates do not dramatically increase or decrease over time.
(B) The various chemicals dissolved in seawater have had the same concentrations over the past million years.
(C) Natural processes unrelated to ice formation do not result in the formation of large quantities of oxygen-18.
(D) Water molecules falling as precipitation usually fall on the open ocean rather than on continents or polar ice packs.
(E) Increases in global temperature do not increase the amount of water that evaporates from the oceans.

22. The passage suggests that the scientists who first constructed a coherent, continuous picture of past variations in marine-sediment isotope ratios did which of the following?
(A) Relied primarily on the data obtained from the analysis of Emilianiís core samples.
(B) Combined data derived from the analysis of many different core samples.
(C) Matched the data obtained by geologists with that provided by astronomers.
(D) Evaluated the isotope-ratio data obtained in several areas in order to eliminate all but the most reliable data.
(E) Compared data obtained from core samples in many different marine environments with data samples derived from polar ice caps.

23. The passage suggests that the scientists mentioned in line 5 considered their reconstruction of past astronomical cycles to be
(A) unreliable because astronomical observations have been made and recorded for only a few thousand years
(B) adequate enough to allow that reconstruction's use in explaining glacial cycles if a record of the latter could be found
(C) in need of confirmation through comparison with an independent source of

笔 记 区

information about astronomical phenomena

(D) incomplete and therefore unusable for the purposes of explaining the causes of ice ages

(E) adequate enough for scientists to support conclusively the idea that ice ages were caused by astronomical changes

Although Victor Turner's writings have proved fruitful for fields beyond anthropology, his definition of ritual is overly restrictive. Ritual, he says, is "prescribed formal behavior for occasions not given over to technological routine, having reference to beliefs in mystical beings or powers," " Technological routine" refers to the means by which a social group provides for its material needs. Turner's differentiating ritual from technology helps us recognize that festivals and celebrations may have little purpose other than play, but it obscures the practical aims, such as making crops grow or healing patients, of other rituals. Further, Turner's definition implies a necessary relationship between ritual and mystical beliefs. However, not all rituals are religious; some religions have no reference to mystical beings; and individuals may be required only to participate in, not necessarily believe in, a ritual. Turner's assumption that ritual behavior follows belief thus limits the usefulness of his definition in studying ritual across cultures.

24. According to the passage, which of the following does Turner exclude from his conception of ritual?

(A) Behavior based on beliefs

(B) Behavior based on formal rules

(C) Celebrations whose purpose is play

(D) Routines directed toward practical ends

(E) Festivals honoring supernatural beings

25. The passage suggests that an assumption underlying Turner' s definition of ritual is that

(A) anthropological concepts apply to other fields

(B) festivals and ceremonies are related cultural phenomena

(C) there is a relationship between play and practical ends

(D) rituals refer only to belief in mystical beings or powers

(E) mystical beings and powers have certain common attributes across cultures

26. It can be inferred that the author of the passage believes each of the following concerning rituals EXCEPT:

(A) Some are unrelated to religious belief.

(B) Some are intended to have practical consequences.

(C) Some have no purpose other than play.

(D) They sometimes involve reference to mystical beings.

(E) They are predominantly focused on agricultural ends.

27. Which of the following best describes the organization of the passage?

(A) Factual data are presented and a hypothesis is proposed.

(B) A distinction is introduced then shown not to be a true distinction.

(C) A statement is quoted, and two assumptions on which it is based are clarified.

(D) A definition is challenged, and two reasons for the challenge are given.

(E) An opinion is offered and then placed within a historical framework.

28. SLOUCH:

(A) stand erect

(B) move unhesitatingly

(C) stretch languidly

(D) scurry

(E) totter

29. CLAIM:

(A) renounce

(B) repeal

(C) deter

(D) hinder

(E) postpone

30. EXPEDITE:

(A) impeach

(B) deflect

(C) resist

(D) retard

(E) remove

31. VALEDICTION:

(A) greeting

(B) promise

(C) accusation

(D) denigration

(E) aphorism

32. FACTORABLE

笔 记 区

(A) absorbent
(B) magnifiabl
(C) simulated
(D) irreducible
(E) ambiguous

33. CONVOKE:
(A) disturb
(B) impress
(C) adjourn
(D) extol
(E) applaud

34. REND:
(A) sink
(B) unite
(C) find
(D) spend
(E) unleash

35. CONTRAVENE:
(A) condescend
(B) embark
(C) support
(D) offend
(E) amass

36. NADIR:
(A) summit
(B) impasse
(C) sanctuary
(D) weak point
(E) direct route

37. ABSTRACT:
(A) deny
(B) organize
(C) elaborate
(D) deliberate
(E) produce

38. MENDACIOUS:

(A) assured

(B) honest

(C) intelligent

(D) fortunate

(E) gracious

SECTION 5

Time-30 minute 38 Questions

$x=y=z$

1.	x^3	XYZ

$x < 0$

2.	$3x^2$	$3x^3$

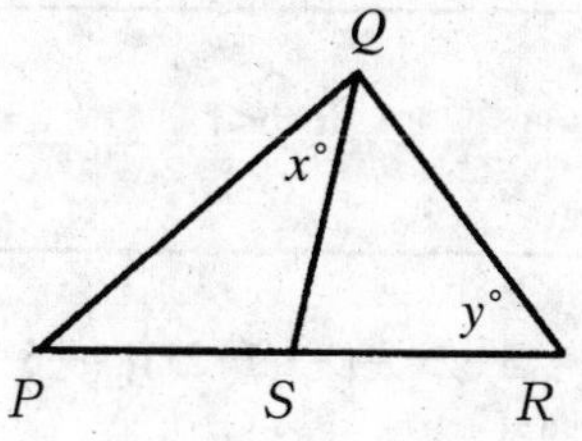

$PS=SR$

3.	x	y

4.	$\frac{24}{23}+\frac{101}{100}$	2

The points P (2,0), Q (0,2), R (4,2) and S (2,4) are in the rectangular coordinate system.

5.	The distance from P to Q	The distance from R to S

The probability that events E and F will both occur is 0.42

6.	The probability that event E will occur	0.58

笔 记 区

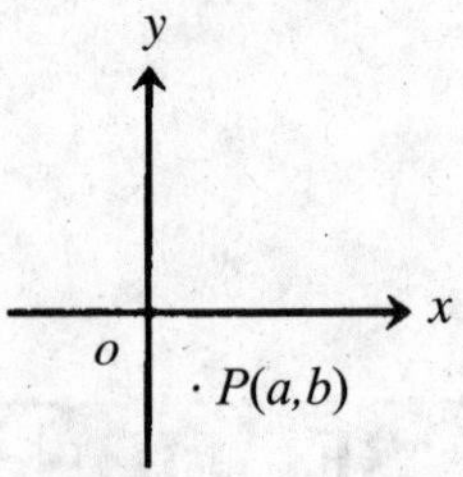

7.	a	b
8.	$(1+\sqrt{2})^2$	3
9.	(109)(87-14)	(109)(87)-(109)(14)

Carol's age, in years, can be expressed by reversing the digits in her father's age, in years. The sum of the digits in each age is 10.

10.	The positive difference between Carol's age, in years, and her father's age, in years	36

$0<p<1$

11.	p^4-p^6	p^3-p^5

$3-2x^2-[-x(1+2x)]=-5$

12.	x	-8

a and b are positive integers.

13.	$\frac{a}{b}$	$\frac{a+3}{b+3}$

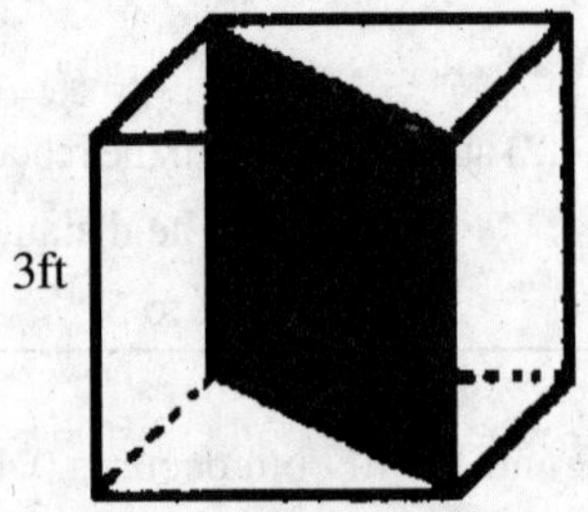

A solid cubical block of wood has dimensions as shown in the figure, and the block is to be cut in half as indicated by the shaded region.

14.	The total surface area of one of the resulting halves of the block	36 square feet

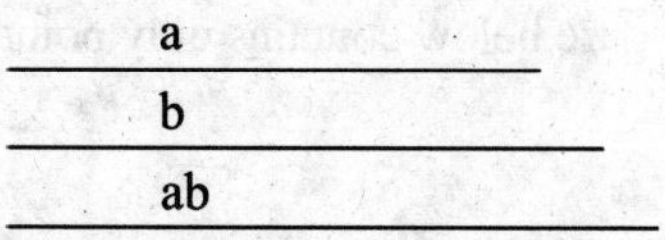

The lengths of the line segments are a, b, and ab, respectively. The line segments are drawn to scale.

15.	a	1

16. The average(arithmetic mean) number of students in 3 economics classes at a certain college is 24. If the total number of students in 2 of the classes combined is 38, how many students are in the remaining class?
(A) 14
(B) 19
(C) 24
(D) 31
(E) 34

17. If the cube of n is 180 greater than the square of n, then n =
(A) 10
(B) 9
(C) 8
(D) 7
(E) 6

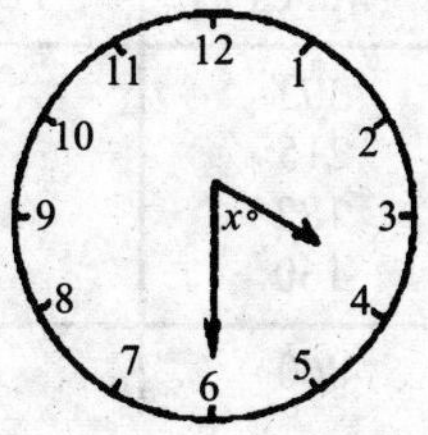

Note: Drawn to scale

18. The circular clock above shows a time of exactly 3:30. What is the value of x?
(A) 60
(B) 75
(C) 85
(D) 90
(E) 105

19. What percent of the integers between 200 and 999, inclusive, end with the digits “03”
(A) 1%
(B) 2%
(C) 3%
(D) 4%
(E) 5%

20. Which of the lines in the figure below contains only points (*x*,*y*) with *x*=*y*?

(A) A

(B) B

(C) C

(D) D

(E) E

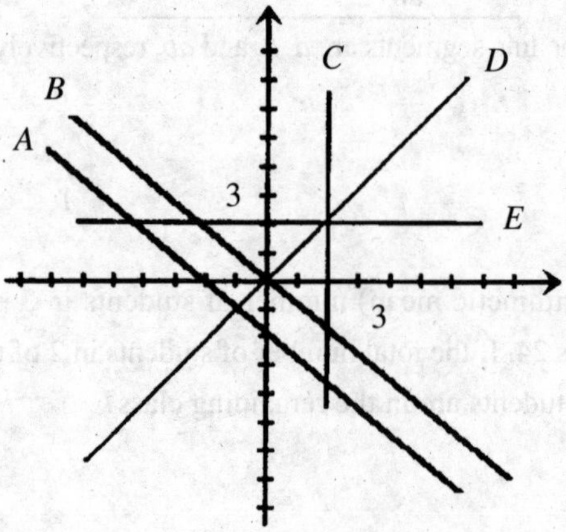

Questions 21-35 refer to the following information about student enrollment in a certain small college.

DISTRIBUTION OF ENROLLMENT
BY CLASS AND SEX
(Total enrollment: 1,400)

	Males	Females
Freshmen	303	259
Sophomores	215	109
Juniors	182	88
Seniors	160	84
Total	860	540

PERCENT OF TOTAL ENROLLMENT
MAJORING IN EACH OF THE FOLLOWING ACADEMIC AREAS
(No student is majoring in more than one area.)

Area	Percent
Humanities	33%
Social Sciences	30%
Physical Sciences	24%

21. The ratio of the number of male freshmen to the number of female sophomores is approximately

(A) 2 to 1

(B) 3 to 1

(C) 3 to 2

(D) 4 to 1

(E) 5 to 3

22. How many of the enrolled students are not majoring in humanities, social sciences, or physical sciences?

(A) 87

(B) 122

(C) 182

(D) 230

(E) 322

23. Which of the following can be inferred from the tables?

Ⅰ. The number of males majoring in physical sciences is greater than the number of females majoring in that area.

II. Students majoring in either social sciences or physical sciences constitute more than 50 percent of the total enrollment.

III. The ratio of the number of males to the number of females in the senior class is less than 2 to 1.

(A) I only

(B) II only

(C) I and II

(D) I and III

(E) II and III

24. How many students are either juniors or males or both?

(A) 678

(B) 766

(C) 948

(D) 1,130

(E) 1,312

25. If the total enrollment is 12 percent greater than it was five years ago, what was the total enrollment five years ago?

(A) 1,180

(B) 1,192

(C) 1,220

(D) 1,232

(E) 1,250

笔 记 区

26. If the ratio of the number of English books to the number of all other books on a bookshelf is 4 to 1, what percent of the books on the bookshelf are English books?

(A) 20%

(B) 25%

(C) 50%

(D) 75%

(E) 80%

3, 7, 9, 14, x

27. The numbers in the list above are ordered from least to greatest. If the average (arithmetic mean) is 2 greater than the median, what is the value of x?

(A) 22

(B) 20

(C) 17

(D) 16

(E) 15

28. A developer has land that has x feet of lake frontage. The land is to be subdivided into lots, each of which is to have either 80 feet or 100 feet of lake frontage. If $\frac{1}{9}$ of the lots are to have 80 feet of frontage each and the remaining 40 lots are to have 100 feet of frontage each, what is the value of x?

(A) 400

(B) 3,200

(C) 3,700

(D) 4,400

(E) 4,760

29. If $\frac{a}{b}=\frac{3}{2}$, which of the following must be true?

Ⅰ $\frac{b}{a}=\frac{2}{3}$

Ⅱ $\frac{a-b}{b}=\frac{1}{3}$

Ⅲ $a+b=5$

(A) Ⅰ only

(B) Ⅱ only

(C) Ⅲ only

(D) Ⅰ and Ⅱ

(E) Ⅱ and Ⅲ

笔 记 区

30. What is the least integer value of *n* such that $\frac{1}{2^n}<0.001$?

(A) 10

(B) 11

(C) 500

(D) 501

(E) There is no such least value.

SECTION 6

Time-30 minute 38 Questions

1. That she was _____ rock climbing did not diminish her _____ to join her friends on a rock-climbing expedition.
(A) attracted to...eagerness
(B) timid about...reluctance
(C) fearful of...determination
(D) curious about...aspiration
(E) knowledgeable about...hope

2. Data concerning the effects on a small population of high concentrations of a potentially hazardous chemical are frequently used to _____ the effects on a large population of lower amounts of the same chemical.
(A) verify
(B) redress
(C) predict
(D) realize
(E) augment

3. Conceptually, it is hard to reconcile a defense attorney's _____ to ensure that false testimony is not knowingly put forward with the attorney's mandate to mount the most defense conceivable for the client.
(A) efforts...cautious
(B) duty...powerful
(C) inability...eloquent
(D) failure...diversified
(E) promises...informed

4. The term "modern" as always been used broadly by historians, and recent reports indicate that its meaning has become more ______ than ever.
(A) precise
(B) pejorative

(C) revisionist
(D) acceptable
(E) amorphous

5. He would _____ no argument, and to this end he enjoined us to _____.
(A) brook...silence
(B) acknowledge...neglect
(C) broach...abstinence
(D) fathom...secrecy
(E) tolerate...defiance

6. Originally, most intellectual criticism of mass culture was _____ in character, being based on the assumption that the wider the appeal, the more _____ the product.
(A) unpredictable...undesirable
(B) ironic...popular
(C) extreme...outlandish
(D) frivolous...superfluous
(E) negative...shoddy

7. Surprisingly, given the dearth of rain that fell on the corn crop, the yield of the harvest was ____; consequently, the corn reserves of the country have not been ____.
(A) inadequate...replenished
(B) encouraging...depleted
(C) compromised...salvaged
(D) abundant...extended
(E) disappointing...harmed

8. REPELLENT: ATTRACT::
(A) elastic: stretch
(B) sensitive: cooperate
(C) progressive: change
(D) flammable: ignite
(E) ephemeral: endure

9. ANARCHIST: GOVERNMENT::
(A) legislator: taxation
(B) reformer: bureaucracy
(C) jurist: law
(D) suffragist: voting
(E) abolitionist: slavery

10. ADMONISH: DENOUNCE::
(A) challenge: overcome
(B) reward: praise
(C) control: contain
(D) persuade: convince
(E) punish: pillory

11. JOKE: PUNCH LINE::
(A) sermon: congregation
(B) conceit: allegory
(C) rhetoric: persuasion
(D) conspiracy: arrest
(E) plot: denouement

12. VEER: DIRECTION::
(A) align: connection
(B) filter: contamination
(C) convert: belief
(D) deflect: motivation
(E) substantiate: authenticity

13. REPROBATE: MISBEHAVE::
(A) sycophant: fawn
(B) critic: rebuke
(C) ruffian: tease
(D) cynic: brood
(E) narcissist: covet

14. IMPERVIOUS: PENETRATE::
(A) ineluctable: avoid
(B) ineradicable: damage
(C) boorish: flatter
(D) irrepressible: censure
(E) disruptive: restrain

15. CONSENSUS: FACTIONALISM::
(A) ritual: orthodoxy
(B) reality: plausibility
(C) reason: thought
(D) clarity: confusion
(E) leadership: subordination

笔 记 区

16. MARTINET: DISCIPLINE::
(A) illusionist: misdirection
(B) dilettante: commitment
(C) renegade: allegiance
(D) pedant: learning
(E) hack: writing

Benjamin Franklin established that lightning is the transfer of positive or negative electrical charge between regions of a cloud or from cloud to earth. Such transfers require that electrically neutral clouds, with uniform charge distributions, become electrified by separation of charges into distinct regions. The greater this separation is, the greater the voltage, or electrical potential of the cloud. Scientists still do not know the precise distribution of charges in thunder clouds nor how separation adequate to support the huge voltages typical of lightning bolts arises. According to one theory, the precipitation hypothesis, charge separation occurs as a result of precipitation. Larger droplets in a thundercloud precipitate downward past smaller suspended droplets. Collisions among droplets transfer negative charge to precipitating droplets, leaving the suspended droplets with a positive charge, thus producing a positive dipole in which the lower region of the thundercloud is filled with negatively charged raindrops and the upper with positively charged suspended droplets.

17. The passage is primarily concerned with discussing which of the following?
(A) A central issue in the explanation of how lightning occurs
(B) Benjamin Franklinís activities as a scientist
(C) Research into the strength and distribution of thunderstorms
(D) The direction of movement of electrical charges in thunderclouds
(E) The relation between a cloudís charge distribution and its voltage

18. The passage suggests that lightning bolts typically
(A) produce a distribution of charges called a positive dipole in the clouds where they originate
(B) result in the movement of negative charges to the centers of the clouds where they originate
(C) result in the suspension of large, positively charged raindrops at the tops of the clouds where they originate
(D) originate in clouds that have large numbers of negatively charged droplets in their upper regions
(E) originate in clouds in which the positive and negative charges are not uniformly distributed

19. According to the passage, Benjamin Franklin contributed to the scientific study of

lightning by

(A) testing a theory proposed earlier, showing it to be false, and developing an alternative, far more successful theory of his own

(B) making an important discovery that is still important for scientific investigations of lightning

(C) introducing a hypothesis that, though recently shown to be false, proved to be a useful source of insights for scientists studying lightning

(D) developing a technique that has enabled scientists to measure more precisely the phenomena that affect the strength and location of lightning bolts

(E) predicting correctly that two factors previously thought unrelated to lightning would eventually be shown to contribute jointly to the strength and location of lightning bolts

20. Which of the following, if true, would most seriously undermine the precipitation hypothesis, as it is set forth in the passage?

(A) Larger clouds are more likely than smaller clouds to be characterized by complete separation of positive and negative charges.

(B) In smaller clouds lightning more often occurs within the cloud than between the cloud and the earth.

(C) Large raindrops move more rapidly in small clouds than they do in large clouds.

(D) Clouds that are smaller than average in size rarely, if ever, produce lightning bolts.

(E) In clouds of all sizes negative charges concentrate in the center of the clouds when the clouds become electrically charged

Before Laura Gilpin (1891-1979), few women in the history of photography had so devoted themselves to chronicling the landscape. Other women had photographed the land, but none can be regarded as a landscape photographer with a sustained body of work documenting the physical terrain. Anne Brigman often photographed woodlands and coastal areas, but they were generally settings for her artfully placed subjects. Dorothea Langeís landscapes were always conceived of as counterparts to her portraits of rural women.

At the same time that Gilpinís interest in landscape work distinguished her from most other women photographers, her approach to landscape photography set her apart from men photographers who, like Gilpin, documented the western United States. Western American landscape photography grew out of a male tradition, pioneered by photographers attached to government and commercial survey teams that went west in the 1860ís and 1870ís. These explorer-photographers documented the West that their employers wanted to see: an exotic and majestic land shaped by awesome natural forces, unpopulated and ready for American settlement. The next generation of male photographers, represented by Ansel Adams and Eliot Porter, often worked with conservationist groups rather than government agencies or commercial companies, but

笔 记 区

they nonetheless preserved the "heroic" style and maintained the role of respectful outsider peering in with reverence at a fragile natural world.

For Gilpin, by contrast, the landscape was neither an empty vista awaiting human settlement nor a jewel-like scene resisting human intrusion, but a peopled landscape with a rich history and tradition of its own, an environment that shaped and molded the lives of its inhabitants. Her photographs of the Rio Grande, for example, consistently depict the river in terms of its significance to human culture: as a source of irrigation water, a source of food for livestock, and a provider of town sites. Also instructive is Gilpin's general avoidance of extreme close-ups of her natural subjects: for her, emblematic details could never suggest the intricacies of the interrelationship between people and nature that made the landscape a compelling subject. While it is dangerous to draw conclusions about a"feminine" way of seeing from the work of one woman, it can nonetheless be argued that Gilpin's unique approach to landscape photography was analogous to the work of many women writers who, far more than their male counterparts, described the landscape in terms of its potential to sustain human life. Gilpin never spoke of herself as a photographer with a feminine perspective: she eschewed any discussion of gender as it related to her work and maintained little interest in interpretations that relied on the concept of a "woman's eye." Thus it is ironic that her photographic evocation of a historical landscape should so clearly present a distinctively feminine approach to landscape photography.

21. Which of the following best expresses the main idea of the passage?
(A) Gilpin's landscape photographs more accurately documented the Southwest than did the photographs of explorers and conservationists.
(B) Gilpin's style of landscape photography substantially influenced the heroic style practiced by her male counterparts.
(C) The labeling of Gilpin's style of landscape photography as feminine ignores important ties between it and the heroic style.
(D) Gilpin's work exemplifies an arguably feminine style of landscape photography that contrasts with the style used by her male predecessors.
(E) Gilpin's style was strongly influenced by the work of women writers who described the landscape in terms of its relationship to people.

22. It can be inferred from the passage that the teams mentioned in line 12 were most interested in which of the following aspects of the land in the western United States?
(A) Its fragility in the face of increased human intrusion
(B) Its role in shaping the lives of indigenous peoples
(C) Its potential for sustaining future settlements
(D) Its importance as an environment for rare plants and animals
(E) Its unusual vulnerability to extreme natural forces

23. The author of the passage claims that which of the following is the primary reason why Gilpin generally avoided extreme close-ups of natural subjects?

(A) Gilpin believed that pictures of natural details could not depict the interrelationship between the land and humans.

(B) Gilpin considered close-up photography to be too closely associated with her predecessors.

(C) Gilpin believed that all of her photographs should include people in them.

(D) Gilpin associated close-up techniques with photography used for commercial purposes.

(E) Gilpin feared that pictures of small details would suggest an indifference to the fragility of the land as a whole.

24. The passage suggests that a photographer who practiced the heroic style would be most likely to emphasize which of the following in a photographic series focusing on the Rio Grande ?

(A) Indigenous people and their ancient customs relating to the river

(B) The exploits of navigators and explorers

(C) Unpopulated, pristine parts of the river and its surroundings

(D) Existing commercial ventures that relied heavily on the river

(E) The dams and other monumental engineering structures built on the river

25. It can be inferred from the passage that the first two generations of landscape photographers in the western United States had which of the following in common?

(A) They photographed the land as an entity that had little interaction with human culture.

(B) They advanced the philosophy that photographers should resist alliances with political or commercial groups.

(C) They were convinced that the pristine condition of the land needed to be preserved by government action.

(D) They photographed the land as a place ready for increased settlement.

(E) They photographed only those locations where humans had settled.

26. Based on the description of her works in the passage, which of the following would most likely be a subject for a photograph taken by Gilpin?

(A) A vista of a canyon still untouched by human culture

(B) A portrait of a visitor to the West against a desert backdrop

(C) A view of historic Native American dwellings carved into the side of a natural cliff

(D) A picture of artifacts from the West being transported to the eastern United States for retail sale

(E) An abstract pattern created by the shadows of clouds on the desert

27. The author of the passage mentions women writers in line 31 most likely in order to
    (A) counter a widely held criticism of her argument
    (B) bolster her argument that Gilpinís style can be characterized as a feminine style
    (C) suggest that Gilpin took some of her ideas for photographs from landscape descriptions by women writers
    (D) clarify the interrelationship between human culture and the land that Gilpin was attempting to capture
    (E) offer an analogy between photographic close-ups and literary descriptions of small details

28. FICTITIOUS:
    (A) classical
    (B) natural
    (C) factual
    (D) rational
    (E) commonplace

29. BRIDLED:
    (A) without recourse
    (B) without restraint
    (C) without meaning
    (D) without curiosity
    (E) without subtlety

30. CAPTIVATE:
    (A) repulse
    (B) malign
    (C) proscribe
    (D) send out
    (E) deliver from

31. DISSIPATE:
    (A) accumulate
    (B) emerge
    (C) overwhelm
    (D) adhere
    (E) invigorate

32. OSTRACIZE:
    (A) clarify

(B) subdue
(C) welcome
(D) renew
(E) crave

33. LOATH:
(A) clever
(B) reasonable
(C) fortunate
(D) eager
(E) confident

34. VITIATE:
(A) ingratiate
(B) convince
(C) regulate
(D) fortify
(E) constrict

35. LAVISH:
(A) insist
(B) criticize
(C) undermine
(D) stint
(E) waste

36. VITUPERATIVE:
(A) complimentary
(B) demagogic
(C) hopeful
(D) admirable
(E) veracious

37. MORIBUND:
(A) discontinuous
(B) natural
(C) nascent
(D) rational
(E) dominant

38. CATHOLIC:

(A) narrow

(B) soft

(C) trivial

(D) calm

(E) quick

六、最新 GRE 笔试模考练习题六

SECTION 1
Time-45 minutes

ISSUE TASK

Present your perspective on the issue you choose from the two topics below, using relevant reasons and /or examples to support your views

Topic 1:

"The concept of 'individual responsibility' is a necessary fiction. Although societies must hold individuals accountable for their own actions, people's behavior is largely determined by forces not of their own making."

Topic 2:

"Society's external rewards are no measure of true success. True success can be measured only in relation to the goals one sets for oneself."

SECTION 2

Time-30 minute

Argument task

Discuss how well reasoned you find this argument.

The following appeared in a memo from the sales manager of Eco-Power, a company that manufactures tools and home appliances.

"Many popular radio and television commercials use memorable tunes and song lyrics to call attention to the products being advertised. Indeed, a recent study of high school students showed that 85 percent could easily recognize the tunes used to advertise leading soft drinks and fast-food restaurants. Despite our company's extensive advertising in magazines during the past year, sales of our home appliances declined. Therefore, to boost company profits, we should now switch to advertisements featuring a distinctive song."

SECTION 3

Time-30 minute 38 Questions

1. We first became aware that her support for the new program was less than______when she declined to make a speech in its favor.
   (A) qualified
   (B) haphazard
   (C) fleeting
   (D) unwarranted
   (E) wholehearted

2. When a person suddenly loses consciousness, a bystander is not expected to_______ the problem but to attempt to_______ its effects by starting vital functions if they are absent
   (A) cure.. precipitate
   (B) minimize.. predict
   (C) determine.. detect
   (D) diagnose.. counter
   (E) magnify.. evaluate

3. The remark was only slightly__________, inviting a chuckle, perhaps, but certainly not a_________.
   (A) audible.. reward
   (B) hostile.. shrug
   (C) amusing.. rebuke
   (D) coherent.. reaction
   (E) humorous.. guffaw

4. Doors were closing on our past, and soon the values we had lived by would become so obsolete that we would seem to people of the new age as_______as travelers from an ancient land.
   (A) elegant
   (B) ambitious
   (C) interesting

(D) comfortable
(E) quaint

5. Ability to_______ is the test of the perceptive historian, a history, after all, consists not only of what the historian has included, but also, in some sense, of what has been left out.
(A) defer
(B) select
(C) confer
(D) devise
(E) reflect

6. Some artists immodestly idealize or exaggerate the significance of their work; yet others,________ to exalt the role of the artist, reject a transcendent view of art
(A) appearing
(B) disdaining
(C) seeking
(D) failing
(E) tending

7. Estimating the risks of radiation escaping from a nuclear power plant is question, but one whose answer then becomes part of a value-laden, emotionally charged policy debate about whether to construct such a plant.
(A) an incomprehensible
(B) an undefined
(C) an irresponsible
(D) a divisive
(E) a technical

8. TREE: FORESTRY::
(A) tractor: agriculture
(B) experiment: laboratory
(C) fuel: combustion
(D) flower: horticulture
(E) generator: electricity

9. COMMAND: REQUEST::
(A) presume: inquire
(B) recommend: propose
(C) summon: invite

笔 记 区

(D) refuse: rebel
(E) authorize: permit

10. PESTLE: GRIND::
(A) whetstone: sharpen
(B) balloon: float
(C) mill: turn
(D) hinge: fasten
(E) switch: conduct

11. ILLITERACY: EDUCATION::
(A) bureaucracy: clarification
(B) oppression: agreement
(C) vagrancy: travel
(D) inequity: redistribution
(E) inclemency: evasion

12. REVERENCE: RESPECT::
(A) resiliency: vitality
(B) appreciation: dependency
(C) avidity: enthusiasm
(D) imagination: creativity
(E) audacity: sentiment

13. APOSTROPHES:WORD::
(A) letters: alphabet
(B) verbs: syntax
(C) ellipses: sentence
(D) commas: punctuation
(E) paragraphs: essay

14. EXAGGERATION: CARICATURE::
(A) craft: art
(B) detail: sketch
(C) illusion: story
(D) brevity: epigram
(E) sophistication: farce

15. MALLEABLE: SHAPE::
(A) apathetic: emotion
(B) irresolute: opinion

笔 记 区

(C) demonstrable: evidence
(D) irredeemable: value
(E) gustatory: taste

16. BOLSTER: SUPPORT::
(A) axis: revolve
(B) spackle: paint
(C) leakage: caulk
(D) heat: insulate
(E) tackle: hoist

Geologists Harris and Gass hypothesized that the Red Sea rift developed along the line of a suture (a splice in the Earthís crust) formed during the late Proterozoic era, and that significant observable differences in the composition of the upper layers of rocks deposited on either side of the suture give clues to the different natures of the underlying igneous rocks.

Other geologists argued that neither the upper rock layer nor the underlying igneous rocks on the one side of the rift differ fundamentally from the corresponding layers on the other side. These geologists believe, therefore, that there is inadequate evidence to conclude that a suture underlies the rift.

In response, Harris and Gass asserted that the upper rock layers on the two sides of the rift had not been shown to be of similar age, structure, or geochemical content. Further more, they cited new evidence that the underlying igneous rocks on either side of the rift contain significantly different kinds of rare metals.

17. Part of the Harris and Gass hypothesis about the Red Sea rift would be weakened if it could be demonstrated that the composition of upper rock layers
(A) cannot cause a suture to develop
(B) has no effect on where a suture will occur
(C) cannot provide information about the nature of underlying rocks
(D) is similar on the two sides of a rift unless a suture divides the two sides
(E) is usually different from the composition of underlying rocks

18. It can be inferred from the passage that the “Other geologists” (line 6) would be most likely to agree with which of the following statements?
(A) Similar geological features along both sides of a possible suture imply the existence of that suture
(B) Sutures can be discovered only where they are not obscured by superimposed geological features.
(C) The composition of igneous rocks permits prediction of the likelihood of a rift developing through them.

笔 记 区

(D) It is possible to date igneous rocks by carefully studying the different kinds of rare metals contained in them and by observing their similarity to the layer of rock that lies above them.

(E) The existence of rock layers on one side of a rift that are similar in composition to rock layers on the other side suggests that no suture exists between the two sides.

19. It can be inferred from the passage that Harris and Gass have done which of the following?

(A) Drawn detailed diagrams of the Red Sea rift.

(B) Based their conclusions on the way in which sutures develop in the Earthís crust.

(C) Rejected other geologists objections to their hypothesis about the Red Sea rift.

(D) Suggested that the presence of rare metals in rocks indicates an underlying suture.

(E) Asserted that rifts usually occur along the lines of sutures

20. According to the passage, Harris and Gass have mentioned all of the following properties of rocks along the Red Sea rift EXCEPT

(A) age of the upper layers of rock

(B) structure of the upper layers of rocks

(C) geochemical content of the upper layers of rocks

(D) metallic content of the underlying igneous rocks

(E) age of the underlying igneous rocks

Proponents of different jazz styles have always argued that their predecessors, musical style did not include essential characteristics that define jazz as jazz. Thus, 1940ís swing was belittled by beboppers of the 1950ís, who were themselves attacked by free jazzers of the 1960ís. The neoboppers of the 1980ís and 1990ís attacked almost everybody else. The titanic figure of Black saxophonist John Coltrane has complicated the arguments made by proponents of styles from bebop through neobop because in his own musical journey he drew from all those styles. His influence on all types of jazz was immeasurable. At the height of his popularity, Coltrane largely abandoned playing bebop, the style that had brought him fame, to explore the outer reaches of jazz.

Coltrane himself probably believed that the only essential characteristic of jazz was improvisation, the one constant in his journey from bebop to open-ended improvisations on modal, Indian, and African melodies. On the other hand, this dogged student and prodigious technicianówho insisted on spending hours each day practicing scales from theory books-was never able to jettison completely the influence of bebop, with its fast and elaborate chains of notes and ornaments on melody.

Two stylistic characteristics shaped the way Coltrane played the tenor saxophone, he favored playing fast runs of notes built on a melody and depended on heavy, regularly accented beats. The first led Coltrane to ìsheets of sound.î where he raced faster and faster, pile-driving notes into each other to suggest stacked harmonies. The second meant that his sense of rhythm was almost as close to rock as to bebop.

Three recordings illustrate Coltraneís energizing explorations. Recording *Kind of Blue* with Miles Davis, Coltrane found himself outside bop, exploring modal melodies. Here he played surging, lengthy solos built largely around repeated motifsan organizing principle unlike that of free jazz saxophone player Ornette Coleman, who modulated or altered melodies in his solos. On Giant Steps, Coltrane debuted as leader, introducing his own compositions. Here the sheets of sound, downbeat accents, repetitions, and great speed are part of each solo, and the variety of the shapes of his phrases is unique. Coltraneís searching explorations produced solid achievement. *My Favorite Things* was another kind of watershed. Here Coltrane played the soprano saxophone, an instrument seldom used by jazz musicians. Musically, the results were astounding. With the sopranoís piping sound, ideas that had sounded dark and brooding acquired a feeling of giddy fantasy.

When Coltrane began recording for the Impulse! label, he was still searching. His music became raucous, physical. His influence on rockers was enormous, including Jimi Hendrix, the rock guitarist, who following Coltrane, raised the extended guitar solo using repeated motifs to a kind of rock art form.

21. The primary purpose of the passage is to
   (A) discuss the place of Coltrane in the world of jazz and describe his musical explorations
   (B) examine the nature of bebop and contrast it with improvisational jazz
   (C) analyze the musical sources of Coltrane's style and their influence on his work
   (D) acknowledge the influence of Coltraneís music on rock music and rock musicians
   (E) discuss the arguments that divide the proponents of different jazz styles

22. The author implies that which of the following would have been an effect of Coltrane's having chosen to play the tenor rather than the soprano saxophone on My Favorite Things?
   (A) The tone of the recording would have been more somber.
   (B) The influence of bebop on the recording would have been more obvious
   (C) The music on the recording would have sounded less raucous and physical
   (D) His influence on rock music might have been less pervasive.
   (E) The style of the recording would have been indistinguishable from that on *Kind of Blue*

23. Which of the following best describes the organization of the fourth paragraph?
   (A) A thesis referred to earlier in the passage is mentioned and illustrated with three specific examples

(B) A thesis is stated and three examples are given each suggesting that a correction needs to be made to a thesis referred to earlier in the passage

(C) A thesis referred to earlier in the passage is mentioned, and three examples are presented and ranked in order of their support of the thesis.

(D) A thesis is stated, three seemingly opposing examples are presented, and their underlying correspondence is explained

(E) A thesis is stated, three dissimilar examples are considered, and the thesis is restated.

24. According to the passage, John Coltrane did all of the following during his career EXCEPT

(A) improvise on melodies from a number of different cultures

(B) perform as leader as well as soloist

(C) spend time improving his technical skills

(D) experiment with the sounds of various instruments

(E) eliminate the influence of bebop on his own music

25. The author mentions the work of Ornette Coleman in the fourth paragraph in order to do which of the following?

(A) Expand the discussion by mentioning the work of a saxophone player who played in Coltraneís style.

(B) Compare Coltraneís solos with the work of another jazz artist.

(C) Support the idea that rational organizing principles need to be applied to artistic work.

(D) Show the increasing intricacy of Coltraneís work after he abandoned bebop

(E) Indicate disagreement with the way Coltrane modulated the motifs in his lengthy solos.

26. According to the passage, a major difference between Coltrane and other jazz musicians was the

(A) degree to which Coltraneís music encompassed all of jazz

(B) repetition of motifs that Coltrane used in his solos

(C) number of his own compositions that Coltrane recorded

(D) indifference Coltrane maintained to musical technique

(E) importance Coltrane placed on rhythm in jazz

27. In terms of its tone and form, the passage can best be characterized as

(A) dogmatic explanation

(B) indignant denial

(C) enthusiastic praise

笔 记 区

(D) speculative study
(E) lukewarm review

28. RECORD:
(A) postpone
(B) disperse
(C) delete
(D) delay
(E) devise

29. EMBED:
(A) induce
(B) extend
(C) extract
(D) receive
(E) diverge

30. WHOLESOME:
(A) deleterious
(B) submissive
(C) provoking
(D) monotonous
(E) rigorous

31. EXTINCTION:
(A) immunity
(B) mutation
(C) inhibition
(D) formulation
(E) perpetuation

32. CURSE:
(A) exoneration
(B) untruth
(C) redress
(D) benediction
(E) separation

33. DECORUM:
(A) constant austerity
(B) false humility

(C) impropriety
(D) incompetence
(E) petulance

34. AGGRANDIZE:
(A) misrepresent
(B) disparage
(C) render helpless
(D) take advantage of
(E) shun the company of

35. VIGILANT:
(A) reluctant
(B) haphazard
(C) gullible
(D) ignorant
(E) oblivious

36. FASTIDIOUS:
(A) coarse
(B) destructive
(C) willing
(D) collective
(E) secret

37. TRACTABLE:
(A) indefatigable
(B) incorrigible
(C) insatiable
(D) impractical
(E) impetuous

38. RESCISSION:
(A) expansion
(B) enactment
(C) instigation
(D) stimulation
(E) abdication

笔 记 区

SECTION 4

Time-30 minute 30 Questions

$$5 \text{ is } \frac{1}{5} \text{ of } x$$

1. x | 1

2. A number whose square is 4 less than twice the square of 10 | 15

$$\sqrt{x-1} = 4$$

3. x | 17

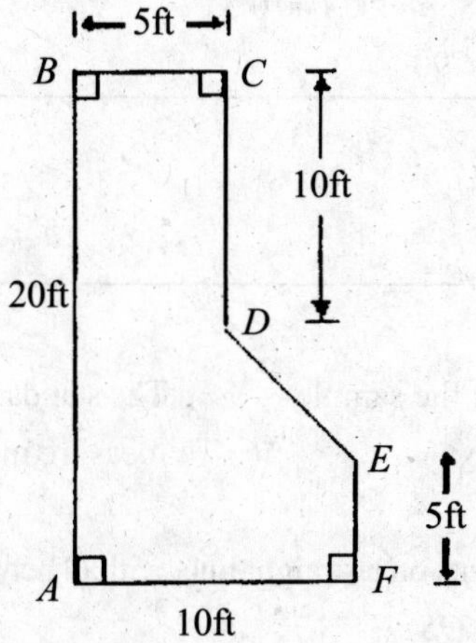

4. The area of region *ABCDEF* | 150 sqft

$$2x = y + 1$$

5. x | y

$$x \neq 0$$

6. $\frac{2}{x}$ | $2x$

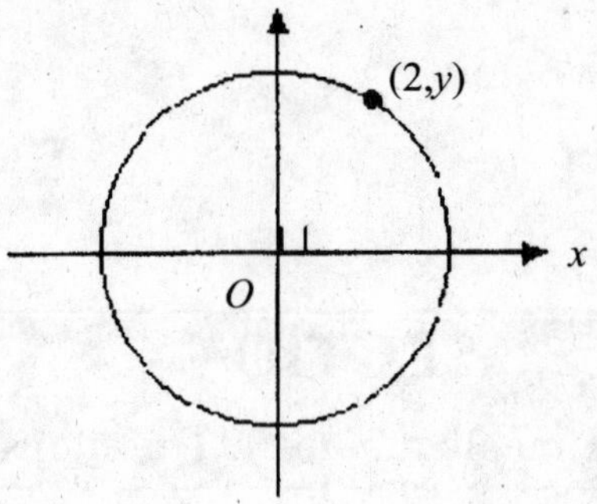

The circle above with center O has a radius of 5

7. y $\sqrt{20}$

A government program paid out $20,000 to each of 60, 000 families.

8. The total amoun that the program paid out to the families $1.2 × 10^9

x and y each represent single digits in the decimal 4.3xy8. When the decimal is rounded to the nearest hundredth, the result is 4.36.

9. x 5

In $\triangle ABC$, $AB = 6$, $BC = 8$, *and* $CA = 10.5$

10. The measure of angle *ABC*90

11. $\frac{4^6-4^4}{4^5-4^3}$ 5

12. The standard deviation of the sample measurements 0, 1, 2,4, 8 The standard deviation of the ample measure ments 1,2,3,5,and 9

P,*Q* and R are distinct points on a straight line, with *Q* between *P* and *R*, *S* is a point not on the line, and $QR = QS$

13. *PR* *PS*

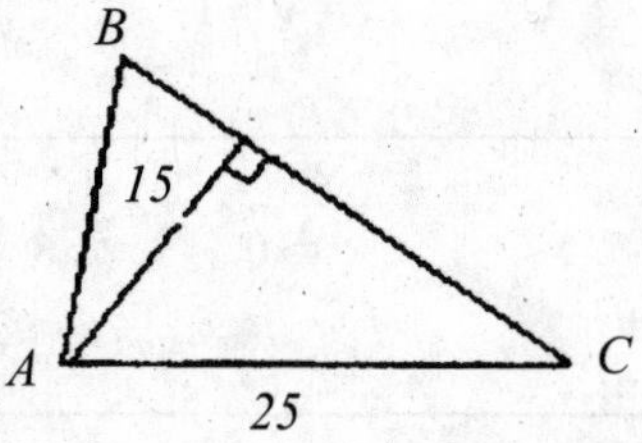

14. The area of triangular region ABC 225

笔 记 区

15. t^3 $\frac{r}{1,000}$

16. Diane completed each of her exercise sets in 25 seconds and rested for 55 seconds between the exercise sets. What is the ratio of the amount of time it took her to complete an exercise set to the amount of time she rested between the sets?

(A) 5:6

(B) 5:11

(C) 6:11

(D) 11:5

(E) 11:6

17. A certain car gets 20 miles per gallon of gasoline for city driving. If the car gets 15 percent more miles per gallon for highway driving, how many miles per gallon does the car get for highway driving?

(A) 17

(B) 22

(C) 23

(D) 30

(E) 35

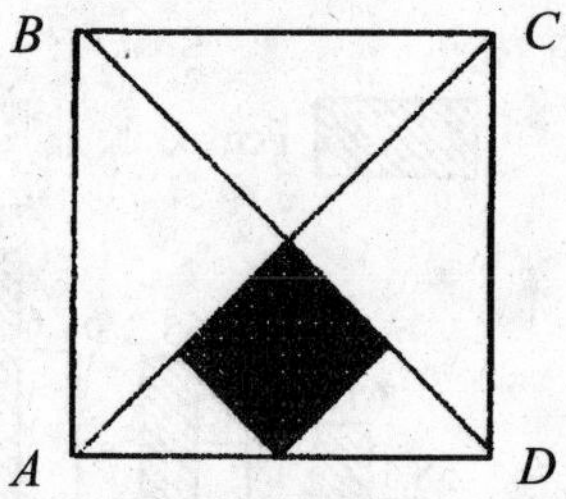

18. In the figure above, the area of the shaded square region is what percent of the area of the square region *ABCD*?

(A) $16\frac{2}{3}$ %

(B) $12\frac{1}{2}$%

(C) 12%

(D) $8\frac{1}{2}$ %

(E) 8%

19. The cost of sending a package special delivery is x cents per ounce up to 10 ounces and y cents for each ounce in excess of 10. Which of the following represents the total cost, in cents, of sending special delivery a package weighing w ounces, if $w > 10$?

(A) $x + (w-10)y + 10$

(B) $x + (w-10) + y$

(C) $10x + 10(w-y)$

(D) $10x + y(w-10)$

(E) $10x+wy$

20. All of the following are equivalent to $\frac{a-b}{c}$ EXCEPT

(A) $\frac{-(a-b)}{c}$

(B) $\frac{-(a-b)}{-c}$

(C) $-\frac{a-b}{-c}$

(D) $-\frac{b-a}{c}$

(E) $\frac{b-a}{-c}$

Questions 21-25 refer to the following graph. In answering these questions, assume that the male and female populations are equal for each of the years shown.

LIFE EXPECTANCY AT BIRTH IN THE UNITED STATES

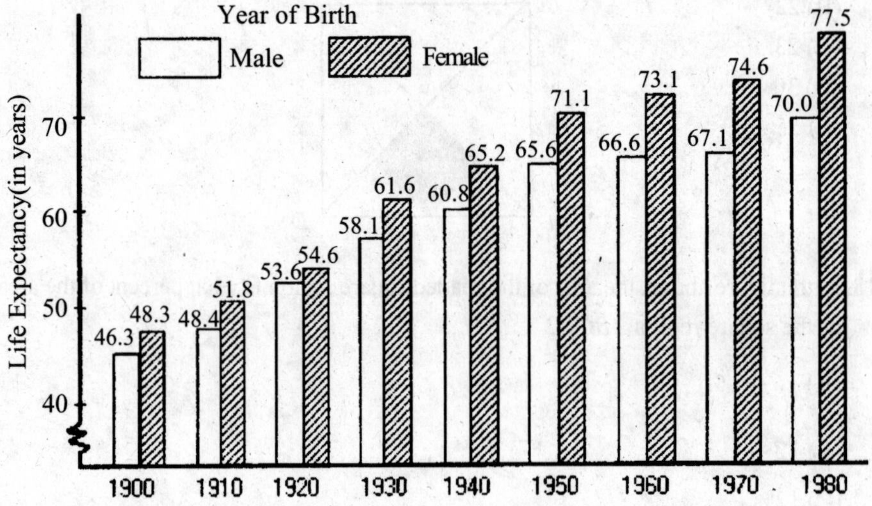

21. For which of the following years was the difference between the life expectancy at birth for males and the life expectancy at birth for females the least?

(A) 1900

(B) 1910

(C) 1920

(D) 1930

(E) 1940

22. The average (arithmetic mean) life expectancy at birth for a person born in 1980 was approximately how many more years than for a person born in 1900?

(A) 20

(B) 22

(C) 24

(D) 26

(E) 30

23. The life expectancy at birth of a male born in 1900 is closest to what fraction of the life expectancy at birth of a male born in 1980?

(A) $\frac{3}{4}$

(B) $\frac{2}{3}$

(C) $\frac{1}{2}$

(D) $\frac{1}{3}$

(E) $\frac{1}{4}$

24. Which of the following statements can be inferred from the graph?

Ⅰ. For each year shown, the life expectancy at birth was greater for females than it was for males

Ⅱ. The increase in the life expectancy at birth for males was greater from 1940 to 1980 than it was from 1900 to 1940.

Ⅲ. For each year shown, the difference between the life expectancy at birth for males and that for females was greater than the corresponding difference in the preceding year shown.

(A) Ⅰ only

(B) Ⅰ and Ⅱ only

(C) Ⅰ and Ⅲ only

(D) Ⅱ and Ⅲ only

(E) Ⅰ, Ⅱ and Ⅲ

25. From 1900 to 1980, life expectancy at birth for males increased by approximately what percent?

(A) 24%

(B) 34%

(C) 40%

(D) 51%

(E) 66%

26. If $\sqrt{7} < x < \sqrt{37}$ and x is an integer, then x can have how many different values?

(A) Three

(B) Four

(C) Five

笔 记 区

(D) Eight

(E) Ten

27. For which of the following expressions is the value for $x = 0$ equal to the value for $x = 1$?

(A) $\frac{X}{X+1}$

(B) $\frac{X+1}{X-1}$

(C) $2x-1$

(D) $x\,(x-1) + x$

(E) $x\,(x-1) +1$

28. It the average (arithmetic mean) of x, y, z, 5, and 7 is 8, which of the following must be true?

I. The median of the five numbers cannot be 5

II. At least one of x, y and z is greater than 9

III. The range of the five numbers is 2 or more

(A) I only

(B) II only

(C) III only

(D) I and III

(E) II and III

29. As shown in the figure above a circular flower bed lies in a square garden plot that is 60 meters on each side. What fraction of the garden plot area is not part of the flower bed?

(A) $\frac{1}{4}$

(B) $\frac{3}{4}$

(C) $\frac{4-\pi}{2}$

(D) $\frac{4-\pi}{4}$

(E) $\frac{\pi-2}{4}$

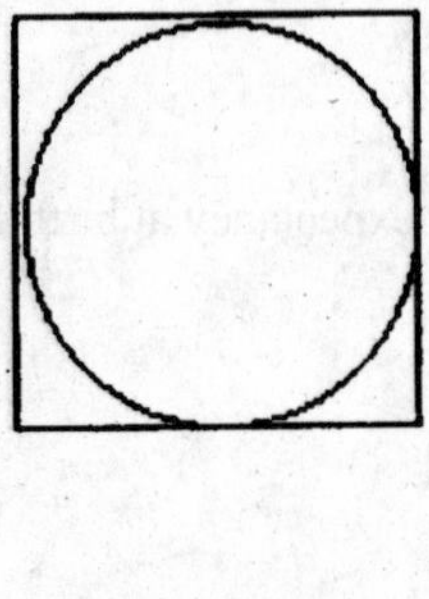

30. Which of the following CANNOT be a factor of 23, where i and j are positive integers?

(A) 6

(B) 8

(C) 27

(D) 42

(E) 54

笔 记 区

SECTION 5

Time-30 minute 38 Questions

1. Because modern scientists find the ancient Greek view of the cosmos outdated and irrelevant, they now perceive it as only of__________interest.
   (A) historical
   (B) intrinsic
   (C) astronomical
   (D) experimental
   (E) superfluous

2. Religious philosopher that he was. Henry More derived his conception of an infinite universe from the Infinite God in whom he believed, a benevolent God of_______whose nature was to create__________
   (A) plenitude ..abundance
   (B) vengeance .. justice
   (C) indifference .. suffering
   (D) indulgence .. temperance
   (E) rectitude .. havoc

3. While some argue that imposing tolls on highway users circumvents the need to raise public taxes for road maintenance, the phenomenal expense of maintaining a vast network of roads__________reliance on these general taxes.
   (A) avoids
   (B) diminishes
   (C) necessitates
   (D) discourages
   (E) ameliorates

4. Although they were not direct__________,the new arts of the Classical period were clearly created in the spirit of older Roman models and thus__________any features of the older style.
   (A) impressions .. introduced

笔记区

(B) translations .. accentuated
(C) copies .. maintained
(D) masterpieces .. depicted
(E) borrowings .. improvised

5. In spite of the increasing_______of their opinions, the group knew they had to arrive at a consensus so that the award could be presented
(A) impartiality
(B) consistency
(C) judiciousness
(D) incisiveness
(E) polarity

6. By forcing our surrender to the authority of the clock systematic timekeeping has imposed a form of__________on society.
(A) anarchy
(B) permanence
(C) provincialism
(D) tyranny
(E) autonomy

7. Our high____________ocabulary for street crime contrasts sharply with our vocabulary for corporate crime, a fact that corresponds to the general publicís unawareness of the extent of corporate crime.
(A) nuanced ..subtle
(B) uninformative ..misleading
(C) euphemistic ..abstract
(D) differentiated ..limited
(E) technical ..jargon-laden

8. DIVERGE : APART::
(A) traverse : across
(B) suspend : around
(C) reverse : beyond
(D) repose : beside
(E) involve : among

9. ATROCIOUS : BAD::
(A) excessive : adequate
(B) momentous : important
(C) unavailing : helpful

笔 记 区

(D) contagious : diseased
(E) nominal : satisfactory

10. PATRONIZE : CONDESCENSION::
(A) exasperate : anger
(B) deride : mockery
(C) compensate : apology
(D) hurry : decision
(E) encroach : fearlessness

11. FANG : TOOTH::
(A) gum : mouth
(B) elbow : arm
(C) bank : river
(D) finger : digit
(E) summit ; mountain

12. ANALGESIC : PAIN::
(A) sedative : sleep
(B) stimulant : mood
(C) antiseptic : odor
(D) anesthetic : sensation
(E) ointment : skin

13. IMPECCABLE : FLAW::
(A) foreseeable : outcome
(B) mundane : substance
(C) dishonorable : blemish
(D) ingenuous : guile
(E) portentous : omen

14. POLEMIC : DISPUTATIOUS::
(A) anachronism : chronological
(B) vernacular : unpretentious
(C) invective : abusive
(D) platitude : insightful
(E) eulogy : unrealistic

15. EMBARRASS : SHAME::
(A) coax : reluctance
(B) sleep : fatigue

(C) doubt : uncertainty
(D) belittle : condescension
(E) console : comfort

16. ETCH : CORROSIVE::
(A) shrink : diminutive
(B) destroy : worthless
(C) glue : adhesive
(D) sculpt : malleable
(E) polish : glossy

A special mucous coating that serves as a chemical camouflage allows clown fish to live among the deadly tentacles of the unsuspecting sea anemone. Utterly dependent on this unlikely host for protection from predators, clown fish have evolved in isolated communities, a pattern that has led to unusual behavioral adaptations.

The rigidly defined hierarchy of each clown-fish community is dominated by a monogamous breeding pair consisting of the largest fish, a female, and the next largest a male, attended by a fixed number of sexually immature fish ranging in size from large to tiny. A remarkable adaptation is that the development of these juveniles is somehow arrested until the hierarchy changes; then they crow in lockstep, maintaining their relative sizes. While the community thus economizes on limited space and food resources, life is risky for newly spawned clown fish. On hatching, the hundreds of larvae drift off into the plankton. If, within three weeks, the defenseless larval clown fish locates a suitable anemone (either by pure chance or perhaps guided by chemicals secreted by the anemone), it may survive. However, if an anemone is fully occupied, the resident clown fish will repel any newcomer.

Though advantageous for established community members, the suspended and staggered maturation of juveniles might seem to pose a danger to the continuity of the community: there is only one successor for two breeding fish. Should one of a pair die, the remaining fish cannot swim off in search of a mate, nor is one likely to arrive. It would seem inevitable that reproduction must sometimes have to halt, pending the chance arrival and maturation of a larval fish of the appropriate sex.

This, however, turns out not to be the case. In experiments, vacancies have been contrived by removing an established fish from a community. Elimination of the breeding male triggers the prompt maturation of the largest juvenile. Each remaining juvenile also grows somewhat, and a minuscule newcomer drops in from the plankton. Removal of the female also triggers growth in all remaining fish and acceptance of a newcomer, but the female is replaced by the adult male. Within days, the maleís behavior alters and physiological transformation is complete within a few months. Thus, whichever of the breeding pair is lost, a relatively large juvenile can fill the void, and reproduction can resume with a minimal loss of time. Furthermore, the new mate has already proved its

笔 记 区

ability to survive.

This transformation of a male into a female, or protandrous hermaphroditism, is rare among reef fish. The more common protogynous hermaphroditism, where females change into males, does not occur among clown fish. An intriguing question for further research is whether a juvenile clown fish can turn directly into a female or whether it must function first as a male.

17. The passage is primarily concerned with
(A) analyzing the mutually advantageous relationship between two species
(B) comparing two forms of hermaphroditism among clown fish
(C) describing and explaining aspects of clown-fish behavior
(D) outlining proposed research on clown-fish reproduction
(E) attempting to reconcile inconsistent observations of clown-fish development

18. It can be inferred from the passage that the clown fish is able to survive in close association with the sea anemone because the
(A) sea anemone cannot detect the presence of the clown fish
(B) tentacles of the sea anemone cannot grasp the slippery clown fish
(C) sea anemone prefers other prey
(D) clown fish does not actually come within the range of the sea anemoneís tentacles
(E) clown fish has developed tolerance to the sea anemoneís poison

19. According to the passage, adult clown fish would be at a disadvantage if they were not associated with sea anemones because the clown fish would.
(A) be incapable of sexual transformation
(B) be vulnerable to predators
(C) have no reliable source of food
(D) have to lay their eggs in the open
(E) face competition from other clown fish

20. It can be inferred from the passage that sex change would have been less necessary for the clown fish if
(A) the male clown fish were larger than the female
(B) each sea anemone were occupied by several varieties of clown fish
(C) many mature clown fish of both sexes occupied each sea anemone
(D) juvenile clown fish had a high mortality rate
(E) both male clown fish and female clown fish were highly territorial

21. The author mentions all of the following as characteristic of the “rigidly defined hierarchy” (line 5) of the clown-fish community EXCEPT:

笔 记 区

(A) At any time only one female clown fish can be reproductively active
(B) The mature clown fish are monogamous
(C) The growth of clown fish is synchronized
(D) The maximum number of clown fish is fixed
(E) There are equal numbers of male juveniles and female juveniles

22. Which of the following statements about newly hatched clown fish can be inferred from the passage?
(A) They develop rapidly
(B) They remain close to the sea anemone occupied by their parents
(C) They are more sensitive to chemical signals than are adult clown fish.
(D) They are not protected by their parents
(E) They are less vulnerable to predation than are adult fish.

23. Which of the following, if true, would be LEAST consistent with the authorís explanation of the advantage of hermaphroditism for clown fish?
(A) The number of individuals in a clown-fish community fluctuates significantly
(B) Adult clown fish frequently cannibalize their young
(C) The sea anemone tolerates clown fish only during a specific stage of the anemone's life cycle.
(D) Juvenile clown fish rarely reach maturity
(E) Clown-fish communities are capable of efficiently recruiting solitary adult clown fish

Comparing designs in music with visual designs raises interesting questions. We are familiar with the easy transfers of terms denoting qualities from one field to another. The basic problem can be put this way: can music sound the way a design looks? The elements of music are not the same as those of painting. They may be analogous, but to be analogous is not to be identical. Is it possible, then, for the same broad characteristics to emerge from different perceptual conditions?

Two facts about the relation between broad characteristics of a work and their perceptual conditions must be kept distinct. First, the global characteristics of a visual or auditory complex are determined by the discernible parts and their relationships. Thus, any notable change in the parts or their relationships produces a change in some of the global characteristics. Second, a change in the parts or their relationships may leave other global characteristics unchanged.

24. In the first paragraph, the author is primarily concerned with establishing the fact that
(A) comparisons are not equations
(B) auditory phenomena are not visual phenomena
(C) frequently used comparisons are usually inaccurate

(D) careless perceptions result from careless thought

(E) questions concerning perception are psychological

25. In the passage, the author is primarily concerned with

(A) distinguishing mutually exclusive categories

(B) clarifying an apparent contradiction

(C) supporting new ideas

(D) analyzing a problem

(E) comparing opinions

26. The second paragraph is primarily concerned with establishing the idea that

(A) different global characteristics of a work result from the same discernible parts

(B) the parts of a work of art influence the total perception of the work

(C) visual and auditory characteristics can be combined

(D) changes in the parts of a work remain isolated from the work as a whole

(E) the visual complexes in a work of art influence the work's auditory complexes

27. Which of the following statements is most likely be a continuation of the passage?

(A) The search for broad similarities thus begins by understanding and distinguishing these two facts.

(B) The search for musical-visual analogies thus depends on the complexity of the works being compared.

(C) The search for music and art of the highest quality thus depends on very different assumptions

(D) Thus music and painting exist in mutually exclusive worlds.

(E) Thus music and painting are too complicated to be evaluated in terms of analogies.

28. COMPRESSION:

(A) increase in volume

(B) change of altitude

(C) loss of stability

(D) absence of matter

(E) lack of motion

29. REFINE:

(A) loosen

(B) obscure

(C) destabilize

(D) decrease size

(E) reduce purity

30. BALK:
(A) extend
(B) derive
(C) observe
(D) plan ahead carefully
(E) move ahead willingly

31. ANTIPATHY:
(A) affection
(B) courtesy
(C) exasperation
(D) obstinacy
(E) cynicism

32. PATHOLOGICAL:
(A) acute
(B) normal
(C) adequate
(D) variable
(E) temporary

33. REIN:
(A) prod
(B) assess
(C) engulf
(D) commend
(E) affirm

34. MELLIFLUOUS:
(A) obtuse
(B) ineffable
(C) raspy
(D) deranged
(E) uproarious

35. IMPUGN:
(A) abandon
(B) anticipate
(C) enable
(D) clarify
(E) endorse

36. PERTINACITY:
   (A) liability
   (B) simplicity
   (C) vacillation
   (D) eccentricity
   (E) misrepresentation

37. GAINSAY:
   (A) speak kindly of
   (B) tell the truth about
   (C) forecast
   (D) affirm
   (E) reiterate

38. ABSOLUTE:
   (A) inferior
   (B) tolerant
   (C) qualified
   (D) preliminary
   (E) immeasurable

笔 记 区

SECTION 6

Time-30 minute 38 Questions

The scale used on a certain map is inch =12 miles.

1. The number of miles represented by 2 inches on the map — 72

2. The number of positive divisors of 24 — The number of positive divisors of 50

$xy = 4$

3. $(2x)(3y)$ — 24

x is an integer greater than 500

4. The value of the integer formed if the order of the digits in x is reversed — 200

A man drove his automobile 10 kilometers in 10 minutes and then drove an additional 15 kilometers in the next 10 minutes.

5. His average speed during 50 kilometers per hour the 20-minute drive

$y > 0$ and $\frac{y}{y-1} > 0$

6. y — 1

7. $\frac{1}{2}+\frac{2}{3}+\frac{3}{4}$ — $\frac{2}{5}+\frac{5}{3}+\frac{3}{8}$

In the rectangular coordinate plane, (x, y) represents a point with coordinates x and y

8. The distance between the points (1,3) and (1,4) — The distance between The points (2,3) and (3,4)

笔 记 区

$$5n + 2 = 7n - 3$$

9. $(\frac{n}{5})^2$ $\frac{1}{5}$

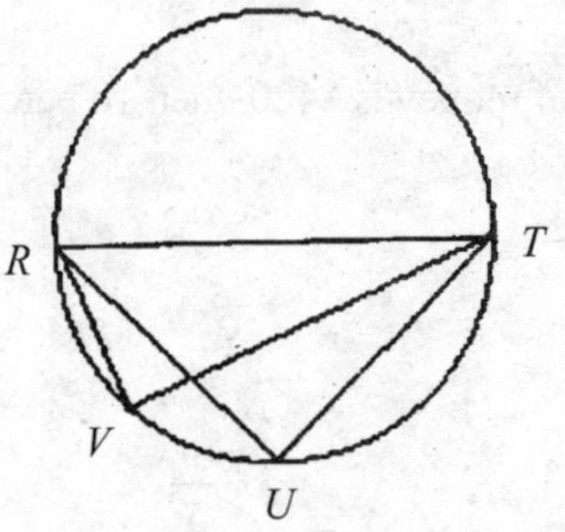

RT is a diameter of the circle above

10. The measure of $\angle RUT$ The measure of $\angle RVT$

11. 2^m $(-2)^m$

$a_k = 1-(-1)^k$, for positive integers k

n is a positive integer

12. a_n a_{n-1}

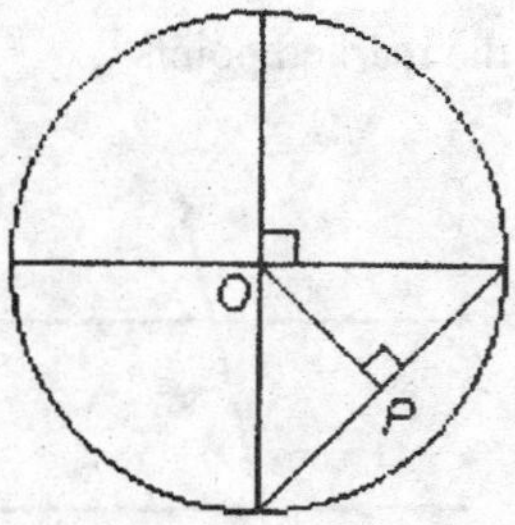

O is the center of a circle of radius r

13. OP $\frac{r}{\sqrt{2}}$

14. The ratio of the area of a circular region with $\frac{3}{5}$ diameter 3 to the area of a circular region with diameter 5

SURVEY OF PETS IN HOUSEHOLDS

IN AN APARTMENT COMPLEX

Kind of Pet	Number of Households
Dog	25
Cat	41
Other	19
No Pet	44

15. The total number of 85

households with at least one pet

16. If 14 percent of an amount of money is \$420, then 10 percent of the same amount is

(A) \$224

(B) \$294

(C) \$300

(D) \$378

(E) \$400

$$n=\frac{k+\frac{r}{s}}{\frac{t}{v}}$$

17. In the equation above, k, r, s, t, and v represent positive numbers. Multiplying which one of these numbers by 2 will reduce the value of n to $\frac{1}{2}$ of its present value?

(A) k

(B) r

(C) s

(D) t

(E) v

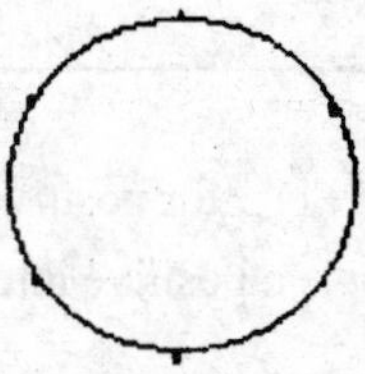

18. There are six marked points on the circle above. How many different lines can be drawn that contain two of the marked points?

(A) 5

(B) 6

(C) 12

(D) 15

(E) 30

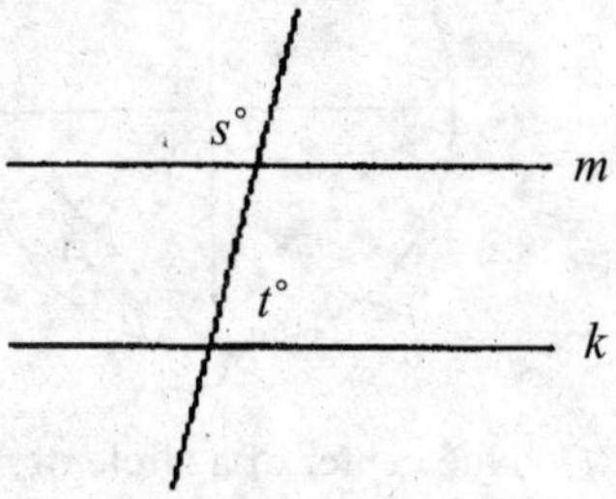

19. In the figure above, if $m \parallel k$ and $s = t + 30$ then $t =$

(A) 30

(B) 60

(C) 75

(D) 80

(E) 105

20. On the real number line, which of the following is halfway between −3.4 and 5.2?

(A) 0.9

(B) 1.2

(C) 1.8

(D) 2.2

(E) 4.3

APPARENT FAHRENHEIT TEMPERATURES DUE TO WIND-CHILL FACTOR

(corresponding to actual temperatures and wind speeds)

WIND SPEEDS (miles per hour)	ACTUAL TEMPERATURES (degrees Fahrenheit)-				
	−10	0	10	20	30
5	−15	−5	7	16	27
10	−13	−22	−9	3	16
15	−45	−31	−18	−5	9
20	−53	−39	−24	10	4
25	−59	−44	−29	−15	1
30	−64	−49	−33	−18	−2
35	−67	−52	−35	−20	−4
40	−69	−53	−37	−21	−5

21. If the actual temperature is 20 degrees Fahrenheit and the wind speed increases from 5 miles per hour to 40 miles per hour, what is the corresponding decrease in the apparent temperature?

(A) 5 degrees Fahrenheit

(B) 24 degrees Fahrenheit

(C) 32 degrees Fahrenheit

(D) 37 degrees Fahrenheit

(E) 44 degrees Fahrenheit

22. If the actual temperature is 13 degrees Fahrenheit and the wind speed is 14 miles per hour, then the apparent temperature could be

(A) 5 degrees Fahrenheit

(B) -12 degrees Fahrenheit

(C) -20 degrees Fahrenheit

(D) -25 degrees Fahrenheit

(E) -32 degrees Fahrenheit

23. If the actual temperature is 30 degrees Fahrenheit and the apparent temperature due to the wind-chill factor is 0 degrees Fahrenheit then the wind speed in miles per hour, must be between

(A) 5 and 10

(B) 10 and 15

(C) 15 and 20

(D) 20 and 25

(E) 25 and 30

笔 记 区

24. At a wind speed of 30 miles per hour, it the actual temperature increases by 10 degrees Fahrenheit then the apparent temperature increases by approximately how many degrees Fahrenheit?

(A) 5
(B) 7
(C) 10
(D) 15
(E) 20

25. Which of the following can be inferred from the table?

I. The apparent temperature for an actual temperature of 20 degrees Fahrenheit and a wind speed of 15 miles per hour is the same as that for an actual temperatrue of 60 degrees Fahrenheit and a wind speed of 40 miles per hour

II. At a constant wind speed as the actual temperature increases the difference between the actual and the apparent temperatures also increases

III. At a constant actual temperature of -10 degrees Fahrenheit the apparent temperature decreases at a constant rate as the wind speed increases

(A) I only
(B) II only
(C) I and III only
(D) II and III only
(E) I, II and III

26. If the sum of two positive integers is 43 and the difference of their squares is 43, then the smaller integer is

(A) 17
(B) 19
(C) 20
(D) 21
(E) 22

27. To obtain an FHA mortgage for $50,000 or more, the home buyer must have a down payment equal to 4 percent of the first $25,000 of the mortgage amount and 5 percent of the portion in excess of $25,000. At settlement the buyer pay a mortgage insurance premium equal to 3 percent of the mortgage amount. What is the maximum FHA mortgage, if any a buyer can obtain if the buyer has only $6,000 available for the down payment and insurance premium?

(A) $62,500
(B) $71,875
(C) $78,125

笔 记 区

(D) $125,00

(E) The home buyer cannot obtain an FHA mortgage

28. If two sides of a triangle have lengths 3.2 and 5.4 then the length of the third side must be between

(A) 0.0 and 2.2

(B) 2.2 and 5.4

(C) 2.2 and 8.6

(D) 3.2 and 5.4

(E) 5.4 and 8.6

29. The odds that a certain event will occur is the ratio of the probability that the event will occur to the probability that it will not occur. If the odds that Pat will win a prize are 4 to 3, what is the probability that Pat will not win the prize ?

(A) $\frac{1}{4}$

(B) $\frac{1}{3}$

(C) $\frac{3}{7}$

(D) $\frac{4}{7}$

(E) $\frac{3}{4}$

30. A certain money market account that had a balance of $48,000 during all of last month earned $360 in interest for the month. At what simple annual interest rate did the account earn interest last month?

(A) 7%

(B) 7.5%

(C) 8%

(D) 8.5%

(E) 9%

笔 记 区

GRE最新笔试模考练习题答案

最新练习题一

SECTION3: BDAEE CEBEA DDBEE BECCD CDBDA DCABD BEECA ABA
SECTION 4: BBAAA ADCDC DCCBD ABBCD DDBDE EAEDE
SECTION 5: CBBAA ACBDC CADBD BCDAC BDECA CDCEB
SECTION 6: EBBEA ECBEB DBBEA EDCCA CCAAC EEEBD ABDDC CCB

最新练习题二

SECTION 3: BCDAD CBDBC CCDCD ADBAB DACEC CEEAE
SECTION 4: EBBCA BBCEE DBBEE BDDED DAABB CCDBB BDCDA EDD
SECTION 5: ADADC DABCD AAABD ADEAE CDCDE CDBBE
SECTION 6: EBCBC DDAAC BADDB CBADE ECCDC DBCCA CEADE EDD

最新练习题三

SECTION 3: BAECD CCEEA CDDCA DBCCC AEBEC ADDBB DDDBE CEE
SECTION 4: CCDBB ACBAD CCABC CBEAB BDBEC EEACE
SECTION 5: BEEBD DACCE EDDAA CCBED CBBCE ADCDB ECBBA DDC
SECTION 6: BAADC ADCDC DBCDB ABEDE CBABD EAEBE

最新练习题四

SECTION 3: EAECC CADBA ADBEE EBCBA EAECA BCAEE CEAAB EDD
SECTION 4: CCCDB CDADB ADCDD CACEE BEBDE DDBAC
SECTION 5: CEEDE CDECD ADCBE BEDBC BCAEA ABEAA DDCAE DBB
SECTION 6: ABABB BDCAC DADDD CCBEC BECDA EEEDB

最新练习题五

SECTION 3: AADBB CADCD ADADD AEDEB DCEBA EDCCB
SECTION 4: BDEAB ACECC BCBAC EAAEE CBBDD EDAAD ADCBC ACB
SECTION 5: CADAC DAACD BCDAA EEBAD BCECE EADDA
SECTION 6: CCBEA BBEED ECAAD DAEBE DCACA CBCBA ACDDD ACA

最新练习题六

SECTION 3: EDEEB BEDCA DCCDB ECECE AAAEB ACCCA EDCBE ABB
SECTION 4: ABCBD DACDA ACADC BCBDA CDBAD BEEDD
SECTION 5: AACCE DDABB DDDCE CCABC EDEAD BAAEE ABACE CDC
SECTION 6: CACDA ABBAC DDCBD CDDCA DBEDA DCCCE

笔 记 区